WRITERS REPUBLIC

Side Effects

The Beach Within

Katia Smith

WRITERS REPUBLIC L.L.C.
515 Summit Ave. Unit R1
Union City, NJ 07087, USA

Website: *www.writersrepublic.com*
Hotline: *1-877-656-6838*
Email: *info@writersrepublic.com*

Ordering Information:
Quantity sales. Special discounts are available on quantity purchases by corporations, associations, and others. For details, contact the publisher at the address above.

Library of Congress Control Number:		2024902726
ISBN-13:	979-8-89100-514-3	[Paperback Edition]
	979-8-89100-516-7	[Hardback Edition]
	979-8-89100-515-0	[Digital Edition]

Rev. date: 03/04/2024

Six-Year-Old Katia

I am trying to write this letter to you again and hoping that I can get through it without walking away from it. The only word that describes you is "scared." You were terrified of the two people who came and took you out of the orphanage and wanted you to call them your mom and dad. They seemed nice enough, with their toys that they would bring you. *I said "you" again*. "Me" is what I meant to say. They brought toys for me. That seemed nice. What they didn't know is that toys were not going to be enough to win me over. It might work on Emma but not on me. I needed to feel. I needed to feel safe and loved. But all you were was scared and afraid of anything and everything that ever tried to do and show you that you are safe. I have given up saying "me" because in a sense, I am writing to an old version of myself. So in a way, I don't know you anymore. I have moved into a big girl's body with adult problems, and yet inside of me, I feel like you—scared of the world and insecure in my own body. I was skin and bones and dying when I came to this country, and that's sometimes how I feel on the inside. When I look in the mirror, I don't recognize the girl looking back at me because I have changed so much—physically, mentally, emotionally, spiritually.

I want to be able to look at us in the mirror and tell you that I love you so much, and yet I won't. I wanted to say "can't," but the truth is, I won't, because I look down on you. I see you as weak and fragile and not strong like Emma. But I am not Emma. I am Katia, and we together as one person is enough. It is easier saying that than believing it. What is wrong with being scared and fragile as a six-year-old in a new country and in a new house with new people all around you. *That is scary!* I can't imagine what you must have been feeling during the first few years of being in America.

I hope you know that I don't blame you for anything anymore. I can see now that you were a little girl trying to stay alive. You had surgery right when you came here and that must have been really scary, I still remember getting out of the car and letting go of the balloon and feeling sad about it. I need to forgive you for being a human and not a perfect robot.

I am sorry for all the years I was so mean to you and looking down on you as if you were nothing. I can see now as I am writing this that you were very brave. But allowing myself to call myself brave is uncomfortable for me. Because the older me knows what we had to go through as the years passed along, and it was not always sunshine for us. We were faced with a lot of challenges, and yet you kept getting up in the morning. You never knew what the day was going to bring, but you were brave enough to get out of bed and face it. So my opinion of us has shifted in a way since I started writing to you. I don't ever want to make us feel like we are not enough again. We were raised in a unique way than most children are, and that is okay, because I don't want to be like someone else. I just want to be me, the complete me, with the good and the bad. I don't want to be perfect anymore. God did not make us to be perfect, but he did perfectly make us in his own vision. So with that being said, I am sorry. I am sorry for not loving you the way I should have and for talking down to you and not lifting you up. I am sorry I made you believe all those negative thoughts. I am sorry for it all—for the things I remember and the things that I don't. Most of all, I am sorry for the fact that you were abandoned. That was not a reflection of you. That was the disease of alcoholism. And this disease has destroyed the world you knew, and it also gave you the opportunity at a new life. Let it all go, Katia. It's okay to put all those rocks down. They are so heavy, and you are so tired. Let them all go. Let yourself to rest in the present. Let yourself be safe and happy in this moment. It's okay. It's okay to be happy, and it's okay to be sad. It's okay to be okay and okay to be not. It is all okay.

Katia Smith

Forty-Five Minutes to Therapy

I am watching Pastor Jason's sermon from Sunday, and I am trying to understand the message. He is talking about humility, and I don't really understand what it is all about. It's hard for me to understand at times what is being said because I don't read the Bible. I want to, and I look at it, and I think about it, but I never do it. So instead of reading the Bible, I am rewatching the sermon, and hopefully, I will pick up something that I didn't on Sunday, because I was crying toward the end of the sermon, but I didn't really understand why I was crying. I couldn't tell you what I was thinking about besides everything from Michael to my sister, to my family, to Sheri, to Book Club, to myself, to my church, and to those overseas. I had so many thoughts regarding everything that is going on in the world and in my own personal world.

I am waiting patiently for time to move faster because I don't want to do therapy today. I know I have so much to say, and I must be honest, and I don't want to be. I don't want to acknowledge that I have not been honest—with anyone, not even myself. I have been smoking THC for the last few weeks on and off, and I am not sorry. I like it. It is helping me get through each day. I need you to hear what I am not saying. I do not *like* that I *need* it. I like it because it is medicine that I need to get through the day. My anxiety and depression are so bad that I am unable to function at a normal level. I am starting to have issues sleeping, eating, exercising, taking my meds, and staying sober—spiritually.

I think that I am not a complete addict. I think that I have issues with alcohol, and I do not wish to ever go back to living a life where I was drinking because I know what it does to my mental health. What does THC do? It calms me down, and I can think clearly about my emotions and my feelings. I am tired of feeling the guilt and shame of what I feel. I am not a bad person for smoking THC. I am not mentally ill because of it. I am a human with mental health problems: PTSD, BPD, trauma, and grief. I struggle with my weight daily. I take medications that may or may not be adding to my weight issues. My self-esteem is short because of where I am in my life. I am trying to stay positive and use my skills and learn how else I can live my life. That is why I am doing the DBT program. I want to commit to a year of working on myself because I have not had that. I have been trying to get better for everyone else and not for myself. I am telling the truth for the first time for myself, not because I have to answer someone but because I am a honest person and value honesty. I am tired of hiding and being sad and depressed. I want to be free and be myself, and if they don't like it, so be it.

I am not going to apologize for being me. I am God's child. I am loved and wanted and needed by those in my life, such as the Book Club. They are my family. They always have been and always will be there for me through the good days and the bad. I don't always have to talk about what I am feeling, but when I want to, they will be there to listen and talk to me through any situation. I look forward to the day that if I do have a child and find the one person that I am supposed to spend the rest of my life with, that they will love me unconditionally, and no, I do not think that asking someone to love you unconditionally is hard. Dogs and cats do it every day with their owners, and we are no different. We need God, and we need him now more than ever, because time is not going to stop and the world is not going to get better overnight. It is going to be a process and a very long journey, but it is a journey that I want to be on, because I am a follower of Jesus. If he can get on that cross and die for my sin, the least that I can do is be a decent person and do my part in this world.

Single Girl

Monday, November 29, 2021

Today is three months since Michael and I broke up. My heart is broken. I miss him every day, and yet my memories are blocked regarding the abuse. I would have stayed in that relationship until it would have killed me, either through his hands or my hands. The only thing that I have left from that relationship is Nala, who is a daily reminder that we did have good times together. But all I am holding on to is the memories of his relapses and the pain he put me through. I can see now that the last three months was me surviving and not really living my life.

I have a feeling like the waves are going to take me under with them, and yet I stay standing raw and alone in the middle of winter. The colder it gets, the harder it is for me to move. My entire body shuts down for hours, where I can't keep my eyes open anymore because it's too painful to feel everything that my body is feeling. The nightmares keep me tossing and turning all night long, only to wake up in the morning to an empty bed and a reminder that you are gone, and I will not see you again. My heart is broken into a million little pieces, and breathing becomes difficult on certain days when all I see is you in my mind.

Today I will have self-compassion for myself, because I may be alone but that is okay. Being alone is not a bad thing; it is the aloneness that is really killing me slowly inside—because I am allowing it to. I feel the pain and let the tears run down my face day in and day out. It is a reminder that my love for you was real. I gave you my heart and only asked for yours back, but what I got in return I did not deserve. My forever love is still out there, with a man that will keep me safe and warm and loved. And when I meet him, I will know because he will be everything you were not. Until I meet this man, I want to work on myself.

I had ran out of reasons to stay. I felt guilty for leaving and but also shameful for staying, even though he broke me first.

Tomorrow is the last day of November, and then my favorite holiday season is around the corner, but we are not going to be together for it. December 16 is your thirty-second birthday, and all I wish for you is sobriety and happiness, even though I am the one that is struggling to stay sober now more than ever, because all I want to do is numb out the pain and the reminder of each new day that you are gone. In my eyes, I gave you the world, and even though I couldn't give you a family, I did bring Nala into your life, and you called us a family. How do you hurt your family like this?

Each time you relapsed, I had to detach with love. Detachment is neither kind nor unkind. It does not imply judgment or condemnation of the person or situation from which we are detaching; it is simply a way that allows us to separate ourselves from the adverse effects that another person's alcoholism can have on our lives. Detachment helps families look at their situations realistically and objectively, thereby making intelligent decisions possible.

Katia, you are strong. You will get through this because you have gone through worse. You must remember the pain you felt when you were with him and how unhealthy you were when you were in the chaos of his alcoholism. You are not his higher power. I pray that God can heal my heart and lead me wherever I am supposed to go. One day you will have self-esteem and self-love. It is a process and a journey, and it will not happen overnight, as it did not take a short time to get to where I am today. You are worth this hard work because you have lived your life for everyone around you and not for yourself. Today is the first day of the rest of your life if you choose to keep putting yourself first instead of living your life for Michael, who abused you physically, emotionally, and mentally for two years. That is not love, Katia. Love is kind and patience, and it does not hurt you.

　　　　　　　　　Katia Smith

THE BEGIN

Wednesday, December 1, 2021

When I was six years old, I was adopted from Tver, Russia, with my sister, Emma, who was eight years old. We were adopted by Sarah and John Smith. Your average couple looking to start a family. They had already adopted one son, Adam, at nine months old and decided they wanted more kids. When they came to get us, they were hesitant as we were older and came with more behavioral issues because of our past trauma of being left on the streets of Russia by our alcoholic parents.

Emma and I were playing outside one night, and when it was time to go inside, the doors were locked, and no one let us back into the house. We ended up sleeping outside under a porch that night. When the morning came, a police officer found us and told us he was bringing us back to our parents. That was a lie. He took us to a hospital/orphanage to get checked out for abuse and neglect. It was after being checked out that we were placed in the orphanage system. Our older sister, Tatyana, came to the orphanage to try to take us back home; but the orphanage refused to return us even though she was of legal age to be our guardian.

The only memories I have of being in the orphanage is my sister taking care of all the children while the caregivers would get drunk while on duty. She would bath the children, and that included me. I once tried to run away from the orphanage with a boy but got caught by the fence. I was then brought inside and physically beaten for my actions. I remember crying a lot and being very scared. At night, we would be locked in a big room with all the beds for the children, being in one room. If you needed to go use the bathroom, you had to do it on the carpet or your bed as the doors would be locked from the outside. If you ended up having an accident through the night, you would be punished the next day by being dragged into the bathroom and left there in the dark.

When I finally was adopted, I was scared and did not understand what was happening. The next thing I knew, I was getting on a plane with two strangers, who I would later learn are my new mom and dad. It was a long flight, and my sister did not want to sit next to our dad because he had a long coat on, and she did not like being around men. I, on the other hand, did not mind and spent most of the flight sitting next to him. As my parents would tell us later, we were malnourished from the amount of time we were on the streets of Russia. While on the plane, I would put the food from the airline in my backpack because I did not know when I would see food again. It would not be until later that I would be walking into a new home full of food.

We arrived at O'Hare airport and drove through the northwest suburbs and onto the street of Highland Avenue. We pulled up in front of a house, and this became my new home. Inside the house was filled with people of all ages. It was overwhelming as I did not speak English or did not know who these people were. It was my first time meeting my extended family. As they all looked at us with curiosity, all I could focus on was that wonderful smell that was coming from the kitchen. *Pizza!* We all gathered in the living room. My sister and I inhaled our food like a pair of stray dogs. Some of the family members even had to leave the room because they could not watch us eat. When I accidently knocked over my Pepsi, I froze in fear as I thought I would be punished for making a mess. My mom cleaned it up and gave me a smile.

The night was getting late, and after a long trip, it was time to head upstairs to see our new bedroom. We each had our own bed, pillow, and PJs. I remember having a nightlight by my bed, and I was glad I wasn't going to be stuck in the dark as I had been for so many nights before.

The next morning we had our first breakfast together. It was oatmeal, and to this day, I am still not a fan. My mom was not happy with the fact that I did not like it. I gave her a hard time about eating it, and she lost her patience with me. Shortly after that, we started school. I went into kindergarten, and my sister went into second grade. We did not know any English, and it would not be until I was thirty years old and having a conversation with my former fifth grade teacher, Diana Kent, that I would find out that the elementary school had a meeting with the staff explaining our situation and how there was going to be two new girls coming to the school who had just gotten adopted from Russia and did not know any English. We were placed with the best teachers. They were patient and kind. I learned my ABCs and my name for the first time. By being around kids my own age, I was able to pick up the language with the assistance of speech therapy and ESL. Bless those teachers who dedicate their careers in helping kids like me learn a second language.

The month was November, and at the time there was a stomach flu going around. I was complaining to my mom about having a stomachache that would come and go. When she called the doctor, they told her not to bring me in as it was probably the flu and there wasn't much they could do for me. As the week went on, my condition became severely worse. My mom brought me into the doctor, and they did an X-ray, and they could see I had pinworms eating through my appendix. They informed my mom I had less than forty-eight hours to live, and they needed to perform an emergency surgery to remove my appendix. The doctors had never seen a case like mine, and I had interns in my room all day long trying to learn from the uniqueness of my case. The surgery was a success, and the pinworms were removed.

From that moment on, I grew up with as much of a normal childhood as anyone else. I started making friends through school and joining sports such as soccer to socialize with other kids. I was a decent student who got good grades but struggled with my speech and English the most. School was never easy for me, as I had to work very hard in learning everything that included things like reading and writing. My mom would have us write sentences out on repeat for hours at end so that we could learn and catch up with the rest of my class. This also included staying inside and working on phonics to be able to read at the pace the other kids were at. While other kids spent their summers playing outside, I would be inside reading. It was not easy, but it was worth it. I was able to communicate with my parents, peers, and my teachers.

Growing up, I was always in trouble. "Grounded" was the word I knew the most. I never seemed to be able to do anything right. Whenever I would do something that my mom did not like or approve of, I would be grounded for weeks or months at a time. It started when I was in middle school and progressed into my years as a high schooler. These were the most difficult years growing up. I started going through puberty at an early age. I got my period when I was in fifth grade. In middle school, I was trying to find my way around having crushes and trying to be around boys. I was never taught how to socialize with boys my age, so that was an area of my life I had to navigate through by myself as I did not feel comfortable talking to my parents about such topics as many middle schoolers do.

BROKEN AND BEAUTIFUL

Sunday, December 5, 2021

Today I woke up, and it was after 9:30 a.m. Church starts in thirty minutes. Fuck! Ugh! Fuck it, I will watch it in bed, even though I really wanted to go. Ugh this pandemic. Okay, you can do this, Katia. *Up.* Get up. Let's go. *Up. Up. Up. Up.* Okay, never mind, I am not going. Pastor Jason wouldn't know if I was there or not. It doesn't really matter. *That is it. Get up.* Feet touch the floor. Okay, here we go. We can do this. Clothes on, check. Bathroom time. Pee…brush teeth (my tooth is still bothering me when I sleep and bite down. I can feel the teeth touching, and it hurts. It is what it is. Moving on.) Do I smell? What day did I shower last? What day is today? Sunday. When did you shower last, Katia? I can't remember. When did I see Noel? We had that great day. We were going to get tacos, but the place was closed and not opening until 3:00 p.m. Oh, noooo, we wanted tacos! Ahhhh! Holding each other close while laughing…okay, okay, that's okay. That is fine. *Now what?* "Fuck." I really wanted to take him for tacos. He drove all this way up to see me and eat tacos! Okay, Katia, you can't change that. The taco place is closed. *Pivot! Emerson.* S! Let's go there. Great food, great bar. Let's go. Sit down. We are grateful that we are sitting in the corner away from the other humans, as Noel had just gone through the experience of having COVID. We were grateful to be with each other and that we were able to change so suddenly and not let it ruin our day. We started off with some appetizer, which was egg rolls. It had the amazing tasteful flavors an egg roll can have with a twist of beef taste as well.

As we sat and talked, we decided both to order a Sprite. I was happy to hear Noel order a Sprite because it allowed me to order the same thing and not feel overwhelmed if he got an alcoholic beverage. I then was able to relax and know that I was not the only one that didn't want to order an alcoholic beverage at 1:00 p.m. We talked about the simple things in life. The things we were grateful for, the good and the bad. As we shared, we saw each other more clearly without an expectation of what the other person was going to say. I was able to put my guard down again and remind myself that I was *safe* with Noel. He was not going to hurt me. He is my friend. He cares about me. He wants the best for me. So I started to share the things that were really on my mind. I explained to him how I have been reading a book about *Why Men Do That* by Lundy Bancroft and how it has become so overwhelming to me to listen to because it has been opening my mind up to what happened to me, what I have been going through my entire life. It was not until I allowed myself to put the wall around myself down that I was able to see that this abuse had taken over my existence. It had swallowed me whole. Therefore, she (me) had no purpose. She (I) was consumed by the abuse.

———————— ◆ — ◆ ————————

Deep breaths. It is 7:27 p.m., and I believe I am having an anxiety attack. I am high, and I am trying to get my thoughts out on paper so you can understand how I am feeling right now. My heart is racing, and my head feels light. Nala is lying behind me. I can see that I am live on Instagram. I can hear Nala licking her butt. I can hear the fan. I don't want to feel like pain of losing Michael. The grief that comes with it is linked to my childhood trauma as well as my adopted upbringing. My entire life has been a connection of abuse in one form or another. When I was six years old, my father molested me. I don't remember it happening to me. I was just informed all my life that it did happen to me. When we first came from Russia, we were placed in therapy where the therapist could translate what we were saying. I shared that I was abused by my birth father. My sister was not. How does this make me feel? Angry, abandoned, alone, dirty, trash, hopeful, loved, wanted, needed, "can't live without you" feeling. I can feel these emotions and know they will not hurt me. I am worth more. I deserve more. I am enough. I am beautiful. I am loved. I

Katia Smith

am wanted. I have a purpose. I belong. I matter. I can be better. I can do better. I can change. I can walk away. I can say no. I can be not okay. I can be angry. I can be sad. I can be alone. I can love myself. I can heal. I can forgive myself. I can let go. I can trust myself. I can be safe with myself physically and emotionally. This is my perfect day. I have accepted myself because God already has. He loves me and cherish me. He wants me to be okay and happy and successful. He gives me hope that better days will come. One day I will be making a difference in this world, and I will come back to this day and remember that it was through Jesus Christ that I was able to save myself from myself. I am enough. I am worth it. I belong. I am wanted and needed and loved. I have the best friends in the entire world! I have a church that supports me and understands that I am not alone and that even though I am broken, I am beautiful and God still loves me because I am me.

What a beautiful gift we are given, knowing that we cannot stay too far and too wide. He will still always be there waiting for you to let him inside your heart and have him as your friend, Father, and King. He has a plan for each and every one of us. He makes no mistakes. He loves you, and he wants to get to know you.

Well, God, here we go. Let's get to know Katia Marie Smith. She is thirty years old. She was born on February 20, 1991 (so they say, shh who knows), and she loves Jesus with all her heart. She knows she is not alone. She knows he is with her each step of the way. He has never left me my entire life. He was there when I was being abused every day of every minute. He gave me strength every morning when I opened my eyes and every night when I closed my eyes to see another day. Come, Lord. Come, come, Lord, come. Oh, come let us adore him. Oh, come let us adore him. Christ, the Lord.

You *will* get that job!

You *will* buy that house!

You *will* graduate!

You *will* get through this storm!

You *will* overcome depression!

You *will* achieve your goals!

You *will* find your soul mate!

You *will* receive everything God has for you!

Say a prayer.

I trust you, God. Me, God! Here I am! Send me.

I repent and ask for forgiveness for all my sins, the big ones and the small ones. God's ways are higher than my ways. I must turn my will over to God and repent and return to the Lord.

Pay attention to God. God comes to us, but we are distracted or busy. The presence of God is in our world and in our lives.

LETTING GO OF RESISTANCE

Monday, December 13, 2021

I am struggling of letting go of Michael and what our relationship was. I have PTSD from the abuse I experienced the last two years. I almost don't want to see Michael as an abuser in my mind because that is what he would want. He would want me to see him as the caring, loving boyfriend who loved me and Nala, but that was not always the case. While we had love for each other, there was also a lot of abuse—physical, emotional, and mental. When Michael relapsed in April, he showed up in the middle of the night and walked into the bedroom as I was sleeping. He startled me. He used his keys to get into the apartment. He was intoxicated. He continued to verbally assault me, calling me a cunt, calling me fat cow, etc. Then he slammed the bedroom door. I tried to ignore the comments and told myself it's just the vodka talking. He went into the living room and turned on the TV, and it was loud. Then he ordered pizza from Muggs at about 1:00 a.m. I was over it and tried to continue to sleep, but the volume of the TV kept me up. I decided to get out of bed and confront him about how high the volume was. I first tried to be gentle with my approach as I knew he was highly intoxicated and did not want to set him off. I asked him to lower the volume, then asked him for his keys. I was not going to allow him to show up in our home again and verbally assault me as he pleased. I knew I did not do anything wrong and deserved to feel safe in my home physically and emotionally.

As I grabbed his keys and started to take them off his key chain, he got up and cornered me in front of the closet. He got close to my face and said, "Who the fuck do you think you are?" I was frozen. I didn't know what to do. I gave his keys back and went into the bedroom. I laid my head down and tried my very best to sleep that night and shut out what just happened to me. I didn't understand. This was the first time that he had gotten physical with me. The one thing that he told me he was never going to do just happened. As the memory of the conversation we had about him unable to ever lay a hand on a woman passed through my mind, I had to open my eyes to the reality of my situation. Katia, you are in an abusive relationship with an alcoholic. I had been attending Al-Anon meetings for a few months at this point, but I didn't know what to do next besides continue sitting in those rooms and listening to what everyone had to say about their own experiences with their qualifiers.

As always, the cycle restarted. He sobered up, and we had sex. We never talked about what he had done to me, and we moved on with our lives as if nothing happened. I could never talk about what had happened. I didn't know how to say to him, "You hurt me…physically" or "You scared me" or "You threatened me." Did I make it all up? Was it not that bad? He didn't punch me or bruised me. He was just superintoxicated, and because he was drunk, he started to become aggressive and violent. I was in such denial about what had happened. I couldn't face it. I didn't want to lose him; he was my everything, my world. Without him, who was I? A nobody. I saw myself as Michael's girlfriend and only that. That is why I worked as hard as I could so we could have everything we wanted, such as a roof over our head and food in our bellies. I had invested so much time into this relationship, and I didn't want to leave because I know what it feels like when people abandon you. We had that in common. I was abandoned at six years old, and he was homeless most of his life. I could not leave him out there to fend for himself. He wouldn't make it. He would die without me, and then I couldn't live with myself if anything happened to him. I excused his behavior to not be bad in my mind, even though at this point I knew I was not safe anymore in my home. I didn't care. I needed and wanted him more than my own safety.

A few more months passed, and things escalated each month. Every thirty days, he would be relapsing, and I would either be dropping him off at a hotel or he would be drinking at the apartment and asking me to buy him booze because I was financially supporting him. He had no respect for my boundaries, by not asking me to pay for his drinking or not drinking in our home. I had no say anymore. I couldn't voice my opinion. I just was a part of the disease at that point. Completely invisible and enabling the behavior, not knowing how to make it stop. I kept wanting to change him and believing that if I could get him to stop drinking, he would change and things would improve. That never happened. I could feel myself disappearing in front of my eyes as the rest of the world was just out there living, and all I was doing was surviving through the day to day of being with an alcoholic.

As the summer ended, my best friend, Charlotte, got engaged in Paris. I was beyond happy for her. The first time I felt happiness in a very long time. I knew in that moment that I had to do something special for her as this was her time to shine and I was going to support her in any way I can. I took some time and decided that I wanted to take her out to brunch to celebrate.

As I spoke to other friends of hers, I realized that I was not the only one that wanted to celebrate this special time in her life, and before I knew it, I was planning and organizing her a surprised brunch with her close's girlfriends. I planned the place and the time and decided to have everyone contribute into a gift basket of different items. I felt alive. I felt purpose. I felt excited. I felt needed and wanted. I was doing something that was so natural to me, for a friend that has been in my life for eighteen years. It was in this moment that I knew that my friendships are my purpose. When the day came to go to brunch, it was the happiest I had felt in two years. She was so surprised and felt so loved, and that is all I wanted for her that day. It was a perfect day full of love, friendships, and laughs. If only I knew that the next day my life was going to turn upside down, I would have held on to the last few moments a little harder.

The next day was Sunday. I woke up wanting to relax and recover as the planning was all done and the fun was still on my mind. As I came out of the bedroom and kissed Michael, I could tell something was off. By this time, he had already relapsed in the past. I was so thankful that I came home to him sober and the memory of the previous day was not ruined by alcohol. Only to find out that my day was about to be ruined by the one thing that I thought I could control.

Michael looked at me and said, "I don't want to fight, but I have to get out of here."

As he said the words, I knew he was going to go drink, and the cycle was about to start all over again. I sat there and allowed those words to soak into my mind. I was over it. I couldn't take it anymore. Not again. This is not happening again. I am done.

I simply asked him, "Have you made up your mind?"

He said, "Yes."

He asked if I wanted the keys, and I said yes, knowing that this was it. I was done. I was not going to allow him to ruin another memory with his drinking.

DEAR MICHAEL

Saturday, December 25, 2021

Michael,

I miss you today. I hate myself for it, and yet here I am, sitting in bed on Christmas morning and all I can think about is you. I hate that this is where we ended up. I tried so hard to be the best GF to you, and yet it was never enough. I was never enough for you. I know that you are sick, and I hope that by me letting you go, you are getting the help that you need and are sober. That is all that I wished for this Christmas, that you are spending the day with your mom and Bob and Daisy and are sober. We miss you all the time, and yet I can't let go of the memories of your relapses that left me feeling sad and empty. Not knowing if you were going to hurt me or love me daily was too much for one person to live with. You used to say everyone leaves, and the truth is everyone leaves because you make it impossible for them to want to stay. I stayed repeatedly and chose you repeatedly, and all you chose was the bottle. It breaks my heart every time I look at Nala and know that you loved her, and yet even she was not enough. I don't know if anyone or anything will ever be enough for you.

I don't want to keep waking up every day and be thinking of you and be reminded that I choose you over my sister. I choose you over my "family," and you made me feel like I was making the right choice every day and that they just didn't understand us. While that might be true, then why was it not enough to keep us together? Why is it that we are not together for Christmas if we loved each other as much as it felt? I feel guilty because you made me feel like I could never leave you. I hate you for that. Yet you left me every opportunity that you had. I bought booze for you, I gave you a place to live, I gave you money and food and love, but what do I have to show for it? *Abuse.* Physical, mental, emotional, spiritual abuse. *I didn't want us to end.* I wanted a future that I created in my head with you. I wanted it all—the home, the love, the family, the happily ever after. I wanted you to be my forever.

And yet here I am Christmas morning typing to you through a computer instead of kissing you good morning and opening presents with you. I don't have a relationship with my family or my sister because of you, and yet a part of me is okay with that because through the ups and downs you and I had, they showed their true colors and really told me through their actions what they think and feel about me, and it fucking sucks. It hurts repeatedly every single day that I have parents that don't love me unconditionally. It hurts knowing that my birth parents were alcoholics who left me on the streets of Russia when I was a child unable to defend myself. It hurts that you were right about one thing…*Everyone does leave. You left.* You left us. You broke my heart. You hurt me. You let me cry and feel alone and abandoned me. How did we go from having meals with your family to strangers? How did I go from feeling like I belonged to being alone? Why was this our story? Why are we no longer together? I know why. It's because you were selfish. You only cared about yourself and your needs. You didn't care about me and what I needed or wanted. If it wasn't about you and your needs, then it didn't matter. So instead of slowly building me up, you slowly broke me down until I had nothing left inside of me besides anxiety, depression, and PTSD.

All I can do now is give it up to God. *You are not my Higher Power, Michael. You are not the King of kings.* You are a man, created in the image of God, and I hope you are taking care of yourself, and my Christmas wish for you is that you find God and Jesus; that you put your guard down and you let them in, because at the end of the day, it is the only thing we can do. They are the only ones that can save us. I can't keep living like this—in your shadow. Please, *God*, take this struggle from me and remind me of what your will is needing from me. I don't know what I am supposed to be doing anymore. I can't feel anything anymore. I want to trust in you and give up my will to you. I have to take care of myself today.

Today I want to do the following:

- take a shower, wash my hair
- clean my apartment (clean sheets)
- spend time with people that love me (Aunt Natalie)
- love myself unconditionally because I am worthy of love

> I am done with feel sorry for myself.
>
> I must start living my life.
>
> I must let you go, Michael.
>
> I will always and forever have love for you in my life.
>
> I hope you find peace and happiness.
>
> I hope you find God and Jesus.
>
> I hope you get sober.

Sunday, December 26, 2021

I sent you an email today. I relapsed today and contacted you. All the negative emotions of being alone on Christmas reminded me that I am looking in all the wrong places for justification for being me. If my family, or you, or your mother doesn't acknowledge me, who am I? I wanted to know where your head is, but will I have justice for the pain that I feel daily? I look to my abusers to reassure me that I am enough, and that is the scary part for me. Who is Katia without any of you? My sister responded to my text, saying, "Merry Christmas. Love you," and I cried. I hadn't heard from her in over a year, and I never thought I would hear from her again, especially after she got married without me present in her wedding. That hurt me in a way I didn't know could. She is my only blood, and now I missed a huge milestone in her life. I don't want us to not have a future because of the choices I had made in my past. I did what I did, and I can't go back and change them. I must accept that I am who I am, and that is okay. And that does not mean I am good or bad; it just means that I am human. My entire life has been making choices for others and what they wanted for me.

I made a choice. I choose Michael, and that choice led me to where I am today. I am a stronger, more independent person. I have moved and started a new life for myself, and even though some days are harder than the others, I must learn how to take of myself for the first time in my life, instead of leaning on others to make me feel good about myself.

Forgiving myself and allowing myself to feel the grief and pain that has shaped me the last thirty years has not been easy for me. I have so many voices and noise in my head of who I should or shouldn't be, that I have a difficult time trusting myself and what is best for me. There is so much more life to live, and the only way I can do that is if I continue to be in the present moment and take my trauma and turn it into a beautiful life. I have the best support system with people that love me unconditionally and want me to succeed. Letting go of the idea of what a family should or shouldn't be has been one of the hardest things I have ever had to do because I don't know what love looks like unless it is abuse.

Abuse is my comfort zone. Survival mode is my comfort zone. Who is Katia when she is not being abused? That is the real question that I look forward to finding out for myself. Stepping out of my comfort zone is forcing myself to see myself in a new way. I am not who I was, and I do not know who I will be. All I know is right now, in this moment, I am going through the grieving process as it appears daily. I am a sensitive person who has a lot of emotions and feels deeply for others. I have been hurt so much in such a short amount of time, and I carry all that pain with me daily. Opening that can of worms for me and facing my trauma head on has been one of the hardest things I have ever done in my entire life.

The amount of trauma I have experienced has shaped the kind of person that I want to become. I want to be able to be authentic and vulnerable about my experiences and be able to heal the open wounds that have created chaos in my life for thirty years. I am willing to let go of the expectations of who I am supposed to be and start being who I am, and that is, a survivor of abuse—physical, emotional, mental, and spiritual abuse. While this is part of my story, it is not who I want to be for the rest of my life. I don't want to keep on suffering through the rest my life. I want to be able to let go of my past and move forward, to live in the present moment and allow myself to feel my emotions as they come up and process them and not allow them to dictate the decisions I make moving forward. I feel like I am finding the inner strength within myself to make changes in my life that I have been afraid to do for so long because I never thought I deserved to live a happy, loving life. Each day I make choices for myself to keep me in the present moment and be able to live a healthy lifestyle. Mental health is so important to me, and it has been a struggle for most of my life. I have had struggles with being a perfectionist, people pleasing, rumination, high expectations, anxiety, and depression. I know how to live struggling in my pain, and living my life with my pain is a new chapter that I am ready to begin.

I think the hardest part will be to have compassion for myself while I am changing and growing, especially with the new year around the corner. I want to focus on myself and develop a relationship with myself. Waking up every morning is a gift, and finding the happiness in each moment is a daily struggle that I will continue to work through as I am healing through thirty years of trauma.

I talked to Michael. It is December 26, 2021. It has been four months, and I finally gave into my addiction and relapsed and talked to him. It was the hardest thing to hear his voice and hearing him living his life without me in it. It was like talking to a stranger, and I finally got the answers that I needed. *Nothing has changed.* Him being sober does not change the past, and because of that, I know it will never change what I need for my future. It was taking a dart through the heart. He is sober, and yet nothing has changed. *Why did I do thaattt?*

What did I think I was going to get from that conversation? An "I am sorry." As if that was going to fix anything. As if him coming to terms with the fact that he assaulted me twice was going to change that it happened? Have I been watching too much TV and analyzing every scene? Prince Charming doesn't exist. I have been wanting to be rescued and wanted and needed for so long that I never wanted to look in the mirror and come to terms that it's going to be just me, myself, and I for a *very, very* long time.

Chain Analysis of Problematic Behaviors:

- Describe the problem behavior: contacting Michael and his mom
- Prompting event: rumination, loneliness, heartbroken, pain.
- Vulnerable: I am alone, and I am not used to processing my own issues within myself without focusing on someone else. I should focus on what *I want or need* to sooth myself instead of reaching out to others to validate my own feelings.

Chain of Events:

1. Lying in bed alone
2. Thinking of Michael
3. Wanting to call him
4. Making the choice to do it
5. Changing my mind
6. Saying "Fuck it"
7. Missing him
8. Wanting to hear his voice

9. Dialing

10. Calling

11. Saying, "Hi."

12. Saying, "It's Katia."

13. Talking for forty-five minutes about the past.

14. Realizing there is no more us.

15. Feeling heartbroken

16. Alone

17. Wanting to drink

18. Calling a support (2)

19. Changing course of action of journaling and working through this exercise.

Consequences:

1. Gives both of us hope that we could work even if that is not the reality.

2. Digging me farther into the hole.

3. Risking my own sobriety.

4. Making my heartbreak even worse.

5. Putting my mental and emotional health at risk.

6. Going backward instead of forward.

7. Giving into the loneliness instead of taking care of myself.

Skills:

- OEA
- Positive supports
- Thought diffusion
- Wise mind
- Play the tape forward
- Self-compassion

- Self-soothing
- Nonjudgment stance
- Journaling
- SEEDS
- Play the tape forward

Prevention plans:

Art

- Stop and switch
- Change of scenery
- Call a friend
- Journaling
- *Do anything, and I mean anything*, besides contacting him or her
- Stay sober

Repair:

It's okay that you slipped and contact him. This does not define you. All you can do now is put it behind you and move forward. You heard his voice, and it was nice, and now you have to take yourself out of this hole and move forward with your life. He is not a part of it anymore. He has hurt you. He has abused you. He is not the one for you. You can miss him and love him and know that you deserve better than this. He can't give you what you need. He is unable to love you in the way that you want him to. I know this hurts, and it's okay that it hurts. It means that you loved him and saw a future with him, but God has a better plan for you.

DAY 1 AGAIN

Monday, December 27, 2021

I have come to terms that yesterday I slipped and contacted Michael because my emotional mind was getting the best of me. I missed him so much over Christmas that I was a mess for two days and straight, and even while talking to him, I knew we could never be together again because all I could picture was the relapses and abuse in my head.

My cousin Chris and I talked this morning, and I was in shock that he still wasn't ready to have me in his life again, as if I did something wrong. He was talking to me in a way that really bothered me, but I let it pass because it was not worth my time explaining to someone who does not understand what it was that we had together. The more that I reach out to the outside world, I am starting to understand that not a lot of people really understand the life with an alcoholic or they are alcoholics who are in denial about the fact that they even have a problem to begin with. I am hoping that year 2022 is a year of healing and growing.

I am tired of living in a fantasy world in my head where everything works out and everyone lives happily ever after. That is not the world that we live in, and it will not be the world for a very long time because humanity is quick to blame and point the finger outward instead of inward. I have my demons like everyone else. That is what makes me human. It is the decisions that I make moving forward that will dedicate the kind of life that I will have for myself. I don't want to lose the kind, loving, generously person that I am; and at the same time, I don't want to be a doormat anymore. I have lived my entire life to please others, and from this moment on, I want to choose myself first. I want to take care of my own health and put my own oxygen mask on before I help those around me. I have been struggling with my depression for so long that I feel like maybe I am lazy, and then I remind myself that I am working through thirty years of trauma on top of being a part of society, and that is not an easy task for anyone, and unless someone walks a mile in my shoes, they will never fully understand the pain and resilience I have had to get me to this point in my life. I have had to sacrifice my own happiness to build other people up; and while I was doing that, I was allowing those around me to shove my face deeper into the ground until I was lying in a hole, curled up, not able to climb up anymore.

I made a choice to leave Michael, and now I must live with that choice. Is it painful? Of course. I love him, and a part of me will always love him. Did we share a life together during a pandemic for two years? Fuck, yes, we did. Did I fight like crazy for us? Yes. Yes. I did, and it was still not enough. I don't know if he will ever truly know the damaged that he caused me because of the actions he took. I don't believe that he is capable because he is so self-centered and can't look outward and take responsibility for his own actions. I went four months without contacting him, and that had been the longest we had ever gone without speaking. I was selfish and wanted to know what he was doing and how he was feeling and to control the situation, because for the first time in four months, I realized I was no longer in control of his sobriety. He was doing the work himself, and I wasn't forcing him to do something he didn't want to do anymore. He is living his own life, and if I truly loved him, I would get the fuck out of the way and let go and let God take over.

I have so many resentments in my life toward everyone who has not understood me and judged me for my feelings. I am coming to terms with the fact that I am the one suffering by not letting go of these feelings and that the longer I hold on to them the more I will suffer in my life. Coming to terms with the fact that I can't change those around me is a challenge for me.

- Mom
- Dad
- Emma

- Alex
- Charlotte
- Ruth
- Brittany
- Michael
- Michael's mom
- Bob
- Chris
- Francine
- Amy
- Mary

LAST DAY OF 2021

Friday, December 31, 2021

Today is New Year's Eve, and I am currently on an Al-Anon meeting while drinking my Irish cream cold brew. I am feeling a little sad today because every morning I wake up feeling as if I am coming out of my intense dreams, and even if I don't remember what they were about, I do remember how I felt during the dreams. When I wake up, I feel overwhelmed and do not want to face the day. I want to be able to change the way I wake up in the morning because I want to see each day as a gift and not as a chore.

What am I proud of in 2021?

- I decided to start attending Al-Anon.
- I stopped having others tell me how to live.
- I made choices and had to learn to live with them.
- I left Michael.
- I got a restraining order.
- I moved.
- I went to a trauma program.
- I got my SEEDS under control.
- I asked for help.
- I let go off my fears.
- I am starting my healing process.
- I started loving myself.

Katia Smith

What do I want to let go of from 2021?

- Unrealistic expectations of others.
- Perfectionism
- Fear of being alone
- Guilt and shame
- Self-hate
- Laziness
- Depression
- Anxiety
- The past
- The future

What are my goals for 2022?

- Start working out and take care of my physical health
- Stop smoking
- Keep attending Al-Anon meetings
- Baby steps
- Not living in fear
- Taking care of myself physically, emotionally, mentally, and spiritually
- Keep moving forward and not living in the past
- Live in the *now*
- Live one day at a time
- Don't go backward. Let go of him. He is not your future.

This New Year is going to be a big one. I am focusing on loving myself every single day. I know this will not be easy, and if I change the way I view the world and my home, I will be able to take baby steps and start living a different kind of life. By having a stronger routine of self-care and cleaning after myself, I will not be waking up feeling negative in the morning. I know this is going to be the hardest things that I will have to do for myself, but I can do it. Healing and recovery are not a linger line, and I will have my ups and downs this year, but if I keep moving forward, God will give me all that I need for this new year. I am hoping that I can be the best version of myself this year and *let go of the past! Let them all go! Stop checking up on them. Stop thinking about them. If they wanted you in their lives, you would be. They do not want you in their lives right now or ever, and that is okay!* You do not have to feel like you are doing something wrong because they are not in your life anymore. You can live your life to the fullest and know that people leave.

You are loved by many. This has been proven in 2021.

- God
- Charlotte
- Natalie
- Eddie and Sheri
- Nala
- Joe
- Ruth
- Brittany
- Veronica
- Jordan
- Quinn
- Myself

NEW YEAR 2022

Monday, January 3, 2022

As the new year begins, I wanted to take a moment to write out some of my goals for the new year as I try to accept the things I cannot change and change the things I can change and to have the wisdom to know the difference.

1. Inner peace and serenity

2. Healthy routine with SEEDS

3. Letting go of negativity

4. Self-love and self-compassion

5. Work on my spiritual relationship with Jesus

6. Self-reflection daily

7. Staying in the present moment

8. Smile more and enjoy each day

9. Expanding my relationships

10. Loving myself every day for the next 365 days

I thought Michael called me last night, so without thinking, I dialed his number and asked if he called me. He said no, and it was bizarre, hearing his voice again. I really thought that I wouldn't speak to him in 2022. It was not the best start to a new year as I was trying to change especially since I had stood in front of my entire church and told them I was a survivor of abuse from an alcoholic. I never thought that would happen, especially not in church. I was feeling stronger and scared at the same time. When I went back to my seat, I couldn't keep the tears from coming down my face. I was feeling extremely vulnerable and raw in that moment.

It has been an up and down few days as I was able to sleep all day on Saturday.

PAIN

Friday, January 7, 2022

I can't stop my dreams from keeping me from all the pain that I have been feeling for the last five months. I am always scared and in pain in my dreams because of the pain that people have caused me throughout my life, and I can't seem to get away from it. I am replaying different situations in my head and expressing emotions that I couldn't when I am awake. I am wanting things to be different, and yet I can't find the right thing to do anymore. I miss Michael every single day, and yet it doesn't change the story of our love and how it ended. The reality of the situation is that I was terrified and exhausted of the relapses and didn't want to live a life where I was scared and afraid of the person I was lying next to. My memories are playing tricks on my mind, and all I can see are the good times that we shared together and the man that I saw a future with. The fact that alcoholism was such a big part of our relationship will never change. I have moments where I picture a life without alcoholism, but things would still be the same because he can't support me and care for me the way that I need someone to.

I care about him so much as a person that I was willing to lose him for him to be able to find sobriety within himself and have a chance at a future with happiness. Hearing his voice allowed me to see that nothing has changed between us. He can't see the pain he caused me, or he doesn't want to, but either way, I am left carrying around the baggage of our past. I haven't been able to take care of myself. Simple things such as showering or brushing my teeth is harder than I ever remember it being together.

If I can get to a place in my mind where I see the importance of taking care of myself, I can finally be able to move forward and see that I am worth the little things. I really want to start working out so that I can get rid of some of this weight that I have been carrying around for so long, but the cold is keeping me from being productive. Instead, I find myself being lazy and depressed. OEA! Opposite to Emotion Action needs to be the one thing that I am focusing on because if I continue allowing myself to stay in this depression, I am not going to move forward.

I must let them all go. They are no longer part of my life and just a memory of my past. I do not deserve to continue suffering because of the choices that I made for myself. I wanted to give Michael and I a second chance. I gave it my all, but it was not enough for him to want to stay sober. I feel like if I let them go, then I will lose a part of myself that defines who I am, and then I will have nothing left within myself. Who is Katia when she is not being abused by the ones she loves? A human being trying to find herself in a world that is constantly changing during this pandemic.

My entire body is sore from sleeping, and I am getting a massage on Sunday to take care of myself and allow myself to relax from all the stress that my body is holding on. I am hoping that this will be the beginning of me taking care of myself for the first time in a while.

While I cannot go back and change the past, I can look back at the last two years and know that I did everything I could to show love to Michael, and because he has an illness, I can detach from him with love and know that I had to do so to keep myself safe. I have dreams about trying to fix things with him, and I know the feeling of fear come with these dreams because I know what history has shown me of what happens when I fix things with him. It will not last, and before I know it, I will not feel safe again. If I don't feel safe, then there is no room for a relationship to be had. My wish for the next two years is that I grow as a person I can trust myself and know that I am doing the right thing by living my life the way that I want to and do things for myself like spend quality time with friends and continue to create a relationship with God and getting to know him and know that he is still going to have me in his arms throughout all the ups and downs that I feel.

Katia Smith

If I begin to start taking baby steps, I will be able to grow as a person and start a new life with the things that I want to do for the first time in my life in a way I am *free*. I am a free person to put my past to rest and move on and not be haunted by the past. I did what I did, and now I must live with it and know that I have loved ones in my life that will be there for me during the bad days and especially on the good days. I feel like my mind is blocking things out, so I don't feel the impact all at once. I feel very numb, and that is why I am struggling with my depression and taking care of myself. Another part of me wants to say it's the weather and even laziness. If I can take the steps to take care of myself daily, I feel like I can change the outcome that I want for myself. By cleaning my apartment and eating healthy food, I can start changing in small ways to have a heathier life.

Things Are Moving Too Fast

Wednesday, January 19, 2022

It's been a few days, weeks since I last did some journaling, and I must say things have changed by a lot. I saw Michael on Saturday. I drove out to Woodstock, and I picked him up from a Starbucks, and we went and checked into a hotel. He bought me coffee, which he has never done, and he also bought chipotle for lunch. I bought the room, and we had sex four times. I enjoyed it, and I enjoyed being with him. He didn't seem like the same person from five months ago. I didn't know if it was because he was sober and living in a sober house or because this is the longest, I haven't seen him. Things have no progressed today. I dropped the restraining order against him, and I have mixed feelings about it. We can now talk freely, and we are back to saying "I love you" to each other. I feel like things are moving too fast, and I don't know how to slow them down. He wants to work things out because I don't think he feels like he will ever have someone like me in his life, someone who will allow him to control me and do whatever it is that he says. While I am glad the court stuff is over, I never thought I would give in to him only five months out of the relationship. In a way I feel like I am going backward and not forward. I need space to figure out what I want out of life, and that may mean to not talk to him or see him, and I need to be strong enough to let him go figure out what he wants for himself and get established. I did him a favor by dropping the restraining order, and I think I did it because I know he doesn't know

Katia Smith

where I live and also he is an hour away without transportation and he can't find me.

Even now I don't know if I made the right decision. In a way I feel like I gave him power again, and the difference now is that I will *not* let him suck me back into the chaos, and if he thinks he can or he will, he has another thing coming to him. I can walk away whenever I want from him, and that is the freedom that I will never let him take away from me. My friends do not approve of my decisions of seeing him, and they are right. It is reckless of me to open this door with him. I still have to take care of myself and put myself first in all things I do moving forward. I don't know how to communicate with him that I am hurting regarding the things that happened while he was drinking and how nothing really has changed especially when he won't take accountability for his actions. I feel like I can't have an honest conversation regarding where we stand because I know that will shut me out if I do so. If that is something that he wants to do, then let it be, because I am not going to be a doormat to him anymore. I am going to speak my mind and say what I want to say, and if he doesn't like it, then he doesn't get me in his life. I am going to play this my way and keep myself safe. I do not want to live with him, and he will get to see me when I chose to and when I choose to. I have to remember that I am in control of myself and no one else is. I also have come this far not to have him control me again. I think no contact for a while is the best thing. I just don't have the heart to say it to him because I am curious and familiar when I am with him. I know I need to be comfortable being alone. I want to learn how to do things for myself and not rely on him to make me feel good about myself. Things will not be the same as they were. I refuse to be around it. I will not be dragged down again. He can take it or leave it. Otherwise, I am walking away and never looking back, which is really what I should be doing as it is. When I tell friends about him, they are like, "I can't believe you saw him," and send me articles about codependency. We share something. We share something deep, and we are the only ones to feel it because we had moments of pure hell that we lived through together, but that does not mean that we are good for each other. I am hoping by the end of the week I will have a better understanding of what I want. Right now, I really do need some time and space to get my head clear, and him calling or texting me and expecting I love yous like he did not abuse me is making it worse. He is not willing to see the demon that lived inside of him. I am ready to let him make his bed and live in it too, because the longer I engage with him, the longer the hook is going to last. Just let him go, Katia! Why can you not let him go!?

Michael,

Today was a big day for be by me, dropping the restraining order, and I am glad that part is behind us, and I need you to know that I am still hurting from the actions that occurred throughout the last two years and especially the last months of our relationship. I need you to know that things are different now and I am different. I am not the same person that I was five months ago, and you are not either. We have grown induvial and learned a lot about ourselves during that time. I learned that I am codependent and have anxiety, depression, PTSD, and trauma from the physical, mental, and emotional abuse you put me through when you were intoxicated. I understand that alcoholism is a disease, and yet it does not excuse the unacceptable behavior you put me through. I need you to know that I will not go backward with you. If you want me in your life, I want things to be different and we are taking things very slow. I feel like in the hotel, all my pain and suffering were thrown to the side because my love for you overtook that day and I wanted to be in your arms and feel you besides me because that is what I had missed the most. *You.* I no longer feel afraid of you, and it took me up to this moment to be able to say that. If this is ever going to work, we need to put the past in the past. I forgive you for the actions and the words that you had said to me over the span of our relationship before I walked away from you. I do not hold it against you and have accepted that your alcoholism is a part of you and always will be. I love you, the person who I was with this last Saturday that was gentle and kind and warm and loving toward me. I do not love the person you become when you drink, and I will never be around that person again. I know you cannot guarantee me that you will never relapse again. That is a reality that I have accepted because I know I am powerless over an alcoholic. With that said, I am giving this up to God and having him take control of what happens between us moving forward. If I am distant or do not answer my phone, do not take it personally. It is probably because I am working on myself and am healing. I do want you in my life, and I want you to be in my life in a healthy way. The first step is feeling physically and emotionally safe with you. Physically, when you are sober, I feel safe. When you are drinking, I do not physically or emotionally feel safe with you. Emotionally, it will have to come with time. I would like to get to know you as a person again and see how things evolve. After we both feel safe with each other, I would like to move on to trust, emotional stability, and, lastly, physical stability. I know trust is hard for you. This is going to take a *long time* for both of us. We have hurt each other very badly in the past, and that does not heal overnight. I know why you do not trust me. I hurt you, and you feel abandoned by each time that I walked away from you. I hope you believe me when I say this. I walked away from the devil that lived inside of you and not the sober person you are today. On an emotional level, I want to be vulnerable with each other and share intimate things with each other and more than "How was your day?" I know you have walls around you that reaches up to the sky, and I understand why you have them. I am hoping once we start trusting each other, we will be able to knock down some of those walls together. And lastly, physical. That means sex. No more sex until we have covered the other steps into this new relationship. I want to *step* into a new start with you because I am no longer acting and going to be treated like *pets* to someone that I love with all my heart. Please take some time to read this and reread it and really think about what I am saying to you. If you still want me in your life, then give me a call, and we will move forward. If this is too much for you, I will respect that and let you go for good. I will not call. I will not text. I will let you go and will love you until the day I die. You have changed me. You have shown me the best and worst parts of you, and at the end of the day, the love I have for you does not change ever. It doesn't matter how many months go by without talking or seeing you. You took a part of my heart with you, and it will always belong to you no matter what happens between us.

Yours always and forever,
With love,
Katia

God

Sunday, February 27, 2022

Ummm, I don't know where to start, to be honest. I have been drinking since Ruth's grandmother's funeral. I relapsed. I am off the wagon. I am in pain. I am not handling letting go of Michel very well. I am trying to move forward and then I keep allowing myself to do things that will take me five steps backward. I keep having these amazing memories being made within the storm of pain. I think I am an addict. I think that I am addicted to a lot of things—Michael, alcohol, weed, attention, death. I think about dying all the time. Daily. I do not want to die. I want to live a life where I am free to be who I am and to be accepted as is. Right now it feels like I can't be. I think this has been a feeling for thirty-one years, and I am finally being honest with myself for the first time in a long time. I need to learn to stand on my own and take care of myself for the first time in a very long time, and that is very uncomfortable for me.

I went wedding-dress shopping with my best friend, Charlotte, and I couldn't talk. I couldn't say more than two words because all I saw was my sister. I looked around the room, and all I could see was that day. That day that we went shopping for my sister's wedding dress. She is my blood. She is my family. She is my best friend in this entire world, and I walked away from her. I chose Michael over her. I chose an abuser over her. I chose pain over her. I chose hell over her. I chose him over her. I have chosen him over so much that in the first time in over two years, I am finally seeing just how much my loved ones sacrificed just to be by my side, and knowing that Charlotte was still by my side through it all showed me just how much our friendship means, and I couldn't talk. I saw my best friend grow up in front of my eyes. Suddenly, she wasn't a kid anymore. She was a woman in love. The kind of love that you couldn't wait to wake up too. The kind of love that keeps you safe and you never have to doubt about trust. Being emotional with each other makes being physical with each other that much better. I look at her, and I am overwhelmed with happiness to see her spin in white. She had me speechless with her beauty. My best friend has found her Prince Charming, and I get to watch her fall in love all over again every single day. So there was hope. There was hope for me that I could find something like that. The thing is that, I never really saw that what I was missing was that relationship within myself.

All right, I took a hit and poured myself a new glass of wine. That was a lot for me say. I am angry, which is a second emotion. It really means I am sad. Letting go of the mask is scary as fuck. Underneath it all, I want love. I want to sit by you at a kitchen table and look deep into your eyes and know that you see what I feel and can grab my hand and make my heart feel whole again. I see it in the eyes of my best friend of over sixteen years. She reaches out to me, and I am so scared of losing her that I will not reach out and give her my hand. She can't catch this pain. I can feel it. I can feel the pain. I feel it every day. I dream in it. I walk in it. Day in and day out I am carrying it within me. I put one foot in front of the other, and I live in the moment of each day because that is all I can do. I look around all day long, and I ground myself. What can I see? What can I touch? What can I hear? What can I smell? What can I taste? It's things like deep breaths and journaling that allows the most vulnerable side of you come out.

I am so sad. My heart is broken. If I am honest, I have felt pain before, but I have never felt a pain like this. I go to church, and each Sunday I want to drop to my knees. I didn't know why. I didn't know until this moment that it is because of this broken heart, which was caused by an addict and love that I am no longer able to feel. I am letting go. I am giving it to God. I have him within me every day, as soon as my eyes opens in the morning till they close at night. Every day in and every day out, he helps me get through the day the way that I need to. Is it perfect? No. Is it messy? *Yes.* I can do this. I can stop. I can go back. I can trust God.

Katia Smith

New Chapter

I am currently in bed at the apartment in New Jersey. I am here for treatment for addiction and mental health. I left home on September 17 and got on a plane and didn't look back. I knew I needed more help than what I could do for myself. So without hesitation, I picked up the phone and asked for it. I went to detox, and on October 1, 2022, I started my healing journey at Legacy. This has been the hardest thing I have done in a very long time. For the first time in my life, I am taking care of myself. Tomorrow, I have court to get the restraining order against Michael for the second time. I am scared shitless of the unknown. He doesn't know that I am doing this. God grant me the strength to get through tomorrow. As you know, I care for him, and yet I must care for myself first. I hate that I am in this position again. Being negative about this is not going to help me. I must do what I must do for myself. Abuse is not love. Michael is very sick, and so am I, and right now I must take care of myself. I must let him go. I must heal myself and focus on myself. Yes, I will miss him and the special moments that we shared together that no one besides the two of us saw. I will miss having a "family" with Nala and him, as I know he loves her. I am nervous because after tomorrow, I can't contact him again for two years, and I pray to God that he will be okay and his higher power will take care of him. I hope that I can be strong and let him go. I pray that the fear in me will flee. I pray that Michael chooses to live just as I have. I will always have love for him and want to see him succeed. We are just not right for each other because we are both sick and he wants me to stay sick with him and I can't. I must let go and walk away; otherwise, I may not survive.

My goals for this month are the following:

- Stay strong.

- Stay sober.

- Stay present.

- No communication with Michael or his mom.

- Learn to start loving myself.

- Learn to start accepting myself.

- Learn to start seeing my self-worth.

- Take care of myself mentally and emotionally.

- Learn more coping skills.

- Use my coping skills.

- Take things one day at a time.

Katia, I know you are going to want to talk to Michael, I know it is going to hurt like hell to follow through with this again, and yet I want you to remember you have been here before, and you made it five months without talking to him. *Learn to love yourself. Learn to move on.* There is so much more to life than trauma and abuse. *You don't have to be sad for the rest of your life.* If you need to cry, that is okay. That is your body cleansing itself. Michael was a big chapter of your life, and yet that book is finished, and it is time to put it back on the top shelf and not open it again. You have rewritten each chapter multiple times, and it always ends the same way—with you heartbroken and alone. Find yourself in your pain and hold on to it. Hold on to the new person you are becoming and don't let her go because you only get one life and you have so many different things you can do with your life. Stay sober and begin this new chapter. Get out of your own way and let God guide you to the person he created you to be. The past is in the past. The future is not here yet. Stay in the present moment, and remember I am proud of you, and even though you don't feel it right now, I know you love yourself just a little bit, and for now that is enough.

What Am I Struggling with Today?

Monday, November 7, 2022

Today marks week 6 in PHP. The first group was with Mark, where we talked about honesty and respect. These two qualities I do not have and hope to have. It took my therapist talking to my dad for me to realize how angry I am inside. I don't know if I am angry with myself or everyone else in the world or even maybe God. I think it was too early to get my dad involved, and yet that is what I do. I get everyone involved before I look at myself first. If it isn't Michael, it's everyone else in my life that I rather look at than myself. I am so fucking tired of myself that I rather point the finger at everyone else besides myself. I am the fuck up. I am the one with the issues. I am the one that makes the bad decisions. I am the one with the fucked up mind. I am the one who must live with myself and my choices. I am the only that has let myself down repeatedly. I am the one with no self-esteem. I am the one without any worth. I am the one with no respect for myself.

I am so fucking pissed off, and I just want to scream at the top of my lungs, and yet I still don't think anyone could hear just how much pain me is inside. Why am I still here, God? What do you want from me? Why do you love me? What is it about me that is worthy enough to be alive? I am so fucking depressed inside, and yet you keep waking me up every morning just to show me just how fucked up I am. Free will is a joke. Why did I have to be molested and left on the streets of Russia? Why was

I abandoned and left to fend for myself on the streets of Russia? Why am I so fucking emotional all the fucking time? I am so sad inside, God. I am so fucking sad. I don't want to be sick anymore. I want to feel happiness and peace, and I don't know how I am supposed to do that when I wake up every single fucking day with the same mind. Everyone tells me to give it time, this too shall pass. But I have been waiting for thirty-one years for this to pass. My mind and body are so tired of feeling this way. Every single day I wake up with the same fucking problems and the same fucking pain, and I am just done, God. I don't know how much more I can take of any of this anymore. I don't want to hurt anyone anymore. I don't want to live anymore. I want all the noises and thoughts and voices in my head to go away. I am begging you to please help me. I have nothing left in me.

I don't understand anything anymore. I don't understand why Michael came into my life. I don't understand why I loved someone who treated me so badly. And yet when he wasn't abusing me, I thought that was what loved looked like. All I have ever wanted was to be accepted and loved. I could never accept myself and love myself and that is the honest-to-God truth. I am all those negative things that everyone thinks I am. I am not trustworthy and a manipulator, just to get external validation from everyone and everything that could possibly take any of this pain away. I should be proud that I am fifty-one days sober, and yet it's such a roller coaster of emotions right now. I want to say that I love Michael, and I miss him, but the truth is that I am never ever going to be loved the way I want to be loved by him. I am such an emotional mess right now. The truth is, I am too scared to kill myself, but I don't want to live with myself anymore. So what am I supposed to do? Keep getting up every day and feeling? Is that my option in this world? Do I sound annoying and whiny and stupid? Probably. And yet this is how I am feeling inside, and I don't think anyone truly understands how lonely feeling like this is. Everyone tells me that this too shall pass, but I don't see the light at the end of the tunnel. I just see trains one after another that hit me like a million rocks. So yeah, I am struggling with a lot today. I want to isolate and shut down and crawl into a hole and lie there until I can slowly disappear. I don't want to do this anymore.

Katia Smith

Letting Go and Acceptance

Wednesday, November 16, 2022

Today started as a good day as I woke up on a positive note and went in for my one-on-one with Ykeisha. We had a good conversation, and after we finished, it was like the chaos found me with Gianna. I got way too involved because that is who I am. I want to fix everything and everyone around me because I can't focus on myself. I need to accept people where they are, especially the people in my own life. I must also accept where I am currently right now in my recovery. I am two months sober today, and I am proud of myself. I have worked hard to get to this spot and working with a sponsor and learning how unmanaged my life has become. I am powerless over myself, alcohol, weed, others; and most importantly, I am powerless against my own mind.

I am currently on a 319 AA meeting, and I am proud of myself for getting on a meeting because today was a hard day seeing as it was stressful with everything that I went through with Gianna. On a positive note, I did get my nails done and decided to be present during group. I had a hard time focusing because no one was talking about anything, so I decided to share and work on my own recovery even those who are sleeping. Hopefully, they took something away from what I had to say. I think I am struggling mentally…and emotionally. I don't have much to say anymore.

GOD

Wednesday, November 23, 2022

I have been up since 4:30 a.m. Last night Jesus came to me. He held me as I cried. He heard me as I yelled. He saw me. He stayed with me. He reassured me. He loves me. I am loved. I have always been loved. I have always had him with me, and yet I have pushed him away for thirty years, not understanding what I was really doing by rejecting his love. I have created so much suffering in my pain because I didn't understand there was a simple solution of letting go and giving it to God. I have it as a photo on my phone saver and couldn't even count how many times I have looked at it, and yet I still pushed and pushed and pulled and tugged and fell and cried. I finally stopped playing the game of tug-of-war with myself. I am letting go of you, Katia, that wants to suffer. I am setting you free back to the devil because I am never going back to you. You are selfish, dishonest, entitled, untrustworthy, manipulative, and not a true follower of Jesus.

November 22, 2022, the day I accepted Jesus as my lord and savior, and my king, my father, my friend. It is nice to meet you. I am Katia. I am broken, lonely, scared, and tired. I worry a lot; but I am still caring, loving, compassionate, giving, loyal, and honest. A whole lot of sadness is mixed in my happiness. I am ready to start building my relationship with Jesus. I think I have been for a while and maybe doing work toward it without realizing.

Today is a new day. Sixty-seven days sober and ready to start this holiday season on a positive note. Today I have my one-on-one with Ykeisha and work and group. This week has been hard so far, but I can

Katia Smith

change it around and allow God to work in miraculous ways. I just spoke with April and told her about what I experienced last night with Noah.

God works in mysterious ways. April and I met in Al-Anon almost two years ago. I have never met her in person, and yet I feel like I have known her my entire life. She has been a huge support system for me, not just as another addict but as a Christian. I have seen God work through her and in her own life in so many ways. She gives me strength and courage to keep going each and every day because we both struggle with mental health, and she has not given up yet. She gives me inspiration just to stay for another day and see what God has in store for the both of us. I look forward to catching up with her every few days.

I am really going to miss Sarah and Little. They are leaving on Friday to start their new chapter, and I want to be strong and give them a good send-off. For the remaining time I have at Legacy. I want to try to stay positive and soak up all the knowledge I can before it is my time to go. I am going home on December 15. Back home to Nala. Back home to my apartment. Back home to a new chapter in my life without Michael. It makes me sad knowing that I have done this before, and yet here I am again. God is funny that way. He let me have my way and *still* got me back on the right path of showing me that Michael is not supposed to be in my life right now and if ever again.

I can only imagine the good God has in store for Nala and me. I must continue building my relationship with God and turning to him when I am feeling negativity come over me. Sadness is part of being human, and yet suffering is optional. Pain is inevitable. Through my pain, I am reaching out to you, Jesus. Through him, anything is possible. He has shown me this through my entire life. Instead of fighting him and blaming him, I am going to start loving and appreciating him just the same way as he cares and loves me every single moment of every single day of my entire life until I take my final breath.

SADNESS

Saturday, November 26, 2022

Today I am trying to allow my emotions to come and go as they please. I had another nightmare last night and woke up feeling extremely overwhelmed with sadness and grief. I read my daily devotions, meditated, and went to a meeting. I am currently on the couch having my DD coffee and breakfast, listening to music and watching scenery on the TV. There is so much beauty is this world, and the devil continues to want to bring me down with him. Last night I almost contacted Michael again. I am so glad that I did not and reached out to support instead. I want to get to a place that when sad things happen, I don't want to reach out to him. I want to be able to handle the stressors of the word without adding him into the mix, because as I know he is a trigger and will just bring me down.

Earlier this week I was saved. I surrendered to Jesus. I had hit my rock bottom, and my entire body froze during group. As I was coming out of it, I knew I was done. I was done trying to be in control of my life. I knew I couldn't do anything else from that moment on. I had to give my will over to God. I think I am going to have to make this decision every day when I wake up until it becomes second nature to me. The last few days I have been feeing sad. I think it's because Sarah and Little left, and I became really close to them. Sarah showed me how to laugh again. I am learning how to be on my own again.

PANIC ATTACK

Saturday, December 3, 2022

Today I had a very bad panic attack. The day started out fine. I had a relaxing morning and even got my nails done. After coming home and starting to watch the *Little Princess* on Netflix, the door opened, and a tech brought in a new roommate, and of course, it was the one person who I didn't want to be in our apartment. I know that sounds mean I just didn't want things to change because I got so lucky with roommates. I know who I like to be around and who I don't, and I am not crazy about this girl. She is loud and obnoxious, and I like things calm. I am also twelve days away from going home. When she left to go to get a vape, she didn't lock the door, and a stranger walked in. After that, I was completely in panic mode. I had a complete anxiety attack, and I am still struggling a little bit with it. I don't think so much that I am angry regarding this situation; I am more upset with the fact that my trauma responses got tapped into. I was out of control of my own body. I am sad, angry, and hurting. I am hurting from all the pain that is still inside me from the past. I am so hurt by Michael and how everything played itself out. I feel like I was let down and disrespected and, overall, just abused; and it makes me sad. It makes me sad that he couldn't love me the way I wanted to be loved. It makes me sad that we couldn't be a family together. It makes me sad that Nala will never see him again. It makes me sad that I will never kiss him again. It makes me sad I will never see him again. I am in a lot of emotional pain.

I think that is all that I have to say for right now. I can't seem to find anymore words to describe how I am feeling. I wish I could hear his voice. I am missing his voice right now even though I know he has no good words to say. I will finish this later. It's too painful to talk about any of this. I have to go meditate and go to bed. Some days are harder than others, and today was just a hard day.

Tuesday, December 6, 2022

Today I had a really hard time waking up because I have not been sleeping very well the last few nights. We got a new roommate that moved in, and since she moved in, shit has been hitting the fan. She left the door unlocked, and a complete stranger walked into the apartment, and today we came back to the apartment, and she had a male client upstairs with her in the room. I feel as if this set me off because of Michael. It just reminded me so much of how many times he was in my apartment and I didn't want him there, how many times my skin crawled at the sight of him. I have a lot of trauma to unpack, and today I tried to get Bri to help me with it, and she totally dismissed me. I don't like someone dismissing me. It makes me feel inadequate and as if I don't matter, and I know that is not true. I do matter and so do my feelings, and when a boundary is crossed, I need to be able to communicate it and allow the correct people, to make sure the issue does not continue. I am having a hard time not wanting to isolate. I just don't want to deal with humans now, and I can't seem to get away from them and their bullshit, which reflects myself and my own bullshit. I have been having inappropriate sex conversations. I have been horny. What can I say? LOL. And yet life keeps on going, and I have to learn to slow the fuck down and give myself room to rest and recover from myself. I am always go, go, go; and when it is time to slow down, I feel like I need to be doing something instead of sitting with my emotions. The fact that life is happening and it is not on my terms is what got me in trouble last time.

I am leaving here in eight days, and that is nothing. I can get through this week, and next week will fly by because I will be busy working and getting adjusted to being home. I am nervous about seeing Matt because he can be a bit aggressive with the sex. I am hoping I can be able to assertively communicate for myself and not rely on him to make me feel better. If I start the program sooner than later, I will be able to stay out of trouble. I am so excited to see Nala! I cannot wait! She is going to freak out when she sees me, and I am going to cry so much. I am coming home, baby girl, and I can't wait to hold you and snuggle with you!

Sheri

Monday December 19, 2022

I came home on Thursday, December 15, from rehab; and I was so happy to be back and see all my friends and loved ones. My dad picked me up from the airport. He dropped me off at Aunt Natalie's house, where Charlotte was waiting for me to surprise me. I grabbed her into my arms and hugged her like I have never done before. I was happy to see that she surprised me. After giving me a gift basket and feeding me soup and taking it all in, we went to my church and saw my pastors, and I spent some time with God. I was feeling so many different emotions. I was crying every five minutes, and the sensory of taking everything in was overwhelming.

After spending some time with the pastors, I got into my car and drove back to Aunt Natalie's house. Charlotte and I chatted for a bit, and then Natalie came home and gave me a big hug and took Charlotte and me into the living room. She sat me down and told me to take a deep breath.

She looked at me and proceeded to tell me that on Tuesday, December 13, Sheri was hit by a train and killed. With tears running my face, I went into shock. I couldn't believe the news that I was hearing. Here I was so happy to be home and starting the next chapter of my life, and the first thing that I hear was that the mother figure in my life is dead.

It has been a few days of processing this news, and I have been up and down. I am ninety-four days sober today. I am in shock. I am sad. I am confused. I am having moments of denial. Sleep is on and off, and so is my eating. I haven't showered, and self-care is harder than ever. I am trying to work, and yet I know I am struggling mentally and emotionally with everything. I am trying to take things one minute at a time and leaning on God through this entire process. I think the hardest part of all of this is that she is just *gone*. I was looking forward to seeing her when I got home; and instead, on Thursday, I am going to her funeral. It doesn't seem real. It doesn't seem fair. It doesn't seem like I am equipped to handle such a loss. I know she is in heaven. I know she is okay, and yet I miss her so much that it hurts. I feel for Natalie and Eddie and her family and everyone that knew how amazing she truly was. I am trying to take things one day at a time, and even that seems hard to do. Now I am taking things one hour at a time. I don't want to work at all. My body wants to sleep and rest and just not function, and yet I am pushing through because that is what Sheri would want me to do. She wouldn't want me to crawl into a ball and not move. She would want me to keep on living and moving forward with my life. And yet I can't seem to bring myself to get past the fact that I will never hear her voice again or hug her or laugh with her. I miss my mom. *This isn't fair.*

DAY 1

Sunday January 1, 2023

Happy New Year, 2023! Well, it is officially here a new year full of new beginnings. Today I went to church, and as we reflected through what 2022 brought, I found the courage to get in front of my entire church family and share how God has been faithful in my life through the last year, getting me through the cycle of Michael and I for the final time, sitting beside me as I drank myself numb, getting me on that plane to New Jersey for three months to go to rehab, and to finally end my 2022 year with the death of Sheri.

Today I saw Eddie, Addison, and William. We had a nice visit, and yet I ignored all the signs that going into the house without Sheri being there was going to be a very hard thing to do. Being in that house without her there made it real. Sheri is gone. Sheri has passed away. Sheri is dead. She got hit by a train and died. This is reality. This is the present moment. This is how I am beginning to process something that logically does not make any sense to me. Sheri is the mother I never had, and yet just like that, she is gone. I miss her so much that it hurts. I miss her so much that the pain is too much to bear. If only I could get one more text from her, one more call, one more smile, one more laugh, or one more hug. That's all. All I want is to know that she is in a better place and at peace. And yet I already know the answer. She is. How do I know this? Because I believe in God. I believe in Jesus. I believe in what the cross stands for. I believe that this world is not our forever place, and it is a secondary home to our eternal resting placing in heaven with God and Jesus. That is where Sheri is. She is having the time of her life. She is laughing and dancing and happy and pain free. I will never forget her, and yet I must continue living because

God is not done with me yet. He is calling me. He is calling on me to put on my armor and suit up for another day. Another day of battle, another day of feeling, another day of living. As hard as it is, I have no choice but to do as he asks because he knows what he has planned for me in this crazy thing we call life. I want to be closer to God. I want to trust God. I want to be emotional with God, and I want to devote my life to him from this moment on until the day I take my last breath. As he has shown me in the last thirty-one years, I cannot do it without him. I cannot be who he wants me to be without walking beside him and trusting that even though I may not understand why things happen, I can understand that he loves me and that I am his daughter.

Even though I lost a mother, I gained a father in the process of my grief. I went to the dog park today and walked and thought about a lot of different things, such as Sheri, Michael, my family, Nala, my future, my past, and everything that isn't really the present moment of being out in nature. I go to the dog park when I am anxious; I knew this. And yet I stuffed all my emotions deep down because I was afraid to feel. I did not have faith that I would be safe with God. I think he showed me today that I am physically, mentally, and emotionally safe with him.

Once I got home and lay down and meditated, I was able to see that I was starting to not feel normal and that a panic attack was coming up. But I was able to ask for help today, from April and Melanie. I ended the day at Melanie's house, and we talked as Charlotte colored. I was amazed how God brought us back together. Today was full of emotions, and yet for the first day of the year, I would say it was pretty eye opening. I must learn, as I go into this next year, to be nice to myself. I must, or otherwise, I will not make it. I am so hard on myself and mean to myself that I will never get to place of loving myself unconditionally if I continue doing the same old behaviors and expecting a different result.

Katia, you are doing a great job and I am so proud of you for showing up every single day and continuing to fight through everything that life has shown you. I can't wait to see what 2023 brings you. You deserve peace, love, joy, and happiness. Even on your harder days such as today, never give up on yourself. You are strong. You are loved. You are wanted. You are needed. You are resilient. You are beautiful. You are capable of doing hard things one minute at a time.

DAY 2

Monday, January 2, 2023

Right now it is 10:13 p.m. I am less than two hours away from midnight, and I can put this day behind me and move on to tomorrow. Today I woke up at 4:00 a.m. with panic and was unable to fall asleep until around 8:30 a.m. I woke up around 9:30 a.m. I went over to my parents' house for coffee. We talked about last night and how I had a panic attack. After a while of talking, we decided to go out to eat and had a good meal together.

At the end of the meal, I felt a panic attack coming up. We left and went back to the house. In the car, I called Ally from Legacy and talked to her for about twenty minutes. The anxiety attack passed. I then left and went home where Matt met me, and we had sex. He didn't stay long, which I was fine with because I wasn't feeling the greatest, but it was good to see him. He went on his way, and I eventually was able to get myself together. I went to the 5:00 p.m. meeting, and I am so glad that I did because it was only woman, and I was able to share where I was: physically, mentally, emotionally, and spiritually exhausted and in desperate need of a sponsor.

God answered my prayer, and I found myself a sponsor. I felt like I just belonged there. I felt so much better and was able to get some phone numbers and went back to my parents' house for soup. We talked for a few more hours, and before heading home for the night, I stopped by Aunt Natalie's house. She fed me again, and we watched the *Twilight Zone*.

I am now at home and in bed. *Finally!* I am so tired that I could sleep for a week. I am hoping that I do not fall into a depressed state. I can't worry about that right now. Right now I need to focus on relaxing myself and getting ready to go to sleep. Today was a really hard day and a lot of good happened. I am feeling grateful for my parents, my network, and my friends, and, of course, Nala.

I think about Michael here and there, and it isn't easy for me to address him yet because I have so many negative emotions tied in with him, and yet I pray that he is okay and sober and in a safe place. That is my prayer for him: that he finds God the way I have. Because the whole purpose in life is to find God and have a connection with him, and once you do, life becomes so much easier. I never want to go backward. I want to move forward with my life. I want to be able to move past all of this in time and live in a different way. I want to be able to be the honest person that I know I can be. By allowing myself to be vulnerable and put my guard down, I will feel safe with myself emotionally and start trusting God. I pray in time I will be able to have healthy relationships with myself and others, especially God. I want to give him all of me, and in a way, I guess I already have. I have already surrendered and given my life over to him, and that is all I must do. Sounds like a hard thing to do, and yet my life became so much easier once I did, even on my hardest days such as today. I can do hard things. Today was something hard. I didn't just survive today; I lived it. For the first time in a long time, I feel like I am living. I guess I really was in a coma for thirty-one years and am finally waking up and seeing the world for the first time, and while it is overwhelming because everything is so new, I am also excited to see what the future holds for me and those around me. So far 2023 has been challenging and rewarding, and we are only two days in. LOL. Oh boy, I better strap on as it's going to be a wild ride of healing and recovering, and yet this is everything I have ever wanted for such a long time. And it is finally all coming together one second at a time, one minute at a time, one hour at a time, one day at a time. Good night! Peace and blessings!

DAY 3

Yesterday was not a good day, and it was not a bad day. Yesterday was yesterday, and today is Wednesday, and it is a new day. Three days into the New Year, and I had a blown-out mental breakdown. I woke up at 3:00 a.m. and decided to start my day by doing things around the apartment and letting Nala out and drinking some coffee I was feeling good in the sense that I had no reason to be upset on the fact that I couldn't go back to sleep. Might as well start the day. The only thing was that, I woke up in a sweat and thought that the noise I heard was Michael coming into the apartment with a gun to kill me when really it was just Nala eating her food and her bowl was making noise. From that moment on, I was up and awake. I guess, looking back on it, that was my trauma; and my trauma responses were going of the roof. I was able to stay positive but not really realizing that I wasn't really being positive. I was masking what was going on inside of me and trying to act like everything was fine when really it wasn't.

Waking up feeling like that is not fine and is not normal. I must be able to work through this and be able to address my trauma head on, or otherwise, I will always be stuck in the same patterns. After my anxiety was high, I crashed. I mentally, emotionally, physically, and even spiritually crashed. I was shaking and blocked in the sense that I could hear and yet was not present physically. I ended up calling my dad and telling him I was not okay and that I am suicidal. Why did I say that? 'Cause I think that is how I was feeling in my head. My body didn't want to die, but my brain and my emotions wanted me to die. And sometimes I feel like that is worse than physically wanting to die because you can't always escape it.

The devil is loud, and yet looking back on it, I survived yesterday. I did it. No one else. I did. I told the devil to go fuck himself, and I allowed God into my heart and soul and brain. I allowed him to do what he can only do, and that is to constantly save me from myself.

My dad came over, and we did a therapy section and came up with a plan that I am going to start working at their house and he is going to be my manager. Nala is going to go to doggy day care. I am learning how to take care of myself again physically, mentally, emotionally, and spiritually. I am ready for the challenge. I am scared, and yet I am excited. I want to show myself I can be okay and that I can be healthy. Will it be hard work? Of course. *And yet I can still do hard things.* I am so tired of feeling like shit every day, mentally and emotionally. It has gotten me to my knees and begging God to help me. If I believe and trust God's will to be done and not mine, I will be okay. There is nothing that God can give me that I can't handle. In the last thirty-one years, I have been able to do everything that God has thrown my way and then some. From the streets of Russia to navigating being adopted, to becoming an adult. It has not been an easy ride for me, and it has had a lot of twists and turns, and yet here I am, still alive and breathing and working and functioning like a human being. That is a full-time job all by itself. Throw in a toxic relationship, addiction, trauma, death, and mental health in the equation; and you have a perfect storm of chaos. There is good chaos, and there is bad chaos, and I was comfortable in the negative chaos for so long that I am now learning how to dance with the good chaos; and that is much harder to do, such as self-care, meditating, working, and taking care of my sobriety and mental health and trauma and grief. I can do all these things now. I am taking little steps toward all these things in a positive way and yet the one *big* step I took is surrendering my will over to *God.* That was the only thing I had to do: throw my hands up and say, "You win, God. I need you. I trust you. I love you. I am safe with you. I can be intimate with you. I can have a healthy relationship with you." Why? Because your only Son died on a cross to save me from myself and my sins. And that is something that I can never pay back or need to because I am *saved.* All I had to do is believe and have faith. So, on January 15, when I get baptized, I will know with no hesitation or question that I am a believer in God and Jesus Christ, our Lord and Savior, the only one that could have restored me from sanity.

DAY 4

Wednesday, January 4, 2023

Today was a long day. A good day and yet a very long day. I overslept, because my alarm did not go off. I rushed over to my parents on my first day of working at their house as that is my new office. I felt like I had a hangover because I was so exhausted from the day before. I arrived, and I worked, and I got through the day. I had one panic attack, and I noticed the mini attacks were every twenty to thirty minutes. It was difficult to concentrate and focus on the task at hand, which was work. I was able to pull it together and get through the workday. I went afterward and ran some errands. I had my appointment with Dr. Gibson, and we talked about what had been going on with me the last few days. From his point of view, with the stress of coming home and having a culture shock of not being in treatment and then Sheri getting killed, I went into emotional turmoil and had a mental breakdown because I was no longer regulated. I wasn't sleeping and eating, and in the eyes of SEEDS, I was not doing well. I have not been able to sleep through the night in over three weeks, and my body went into shock. Now that I am a few days away from the first of the New Year, I can see what had happened, and I am not surprised. I am going through a lot. Just like life usually happens, it hit me all at once. I was able to work, food prep, shower, and get a good night sleep. I think the hardest thing for me is that I am feeling sad, very sad.

Why I am sad?

- Sheri passed away
- Michael and I are finished
- Trauma
- Stress at work
- Culture shock
- Struggling taking care of myself and Nala
- Struggling financially
- Struggling with men (sex)
- Self esteem
- Self-worth
- Self-acceptance
- Self-respect
- Self-care
- Self-love
- *And on and on, the list can go.*

Things I Am Proud Of

- ✓ Getting out of bed in the morning
- ✓ Showering at night (self-care)
- ✓ Working
- ✓ Breathing
- ✓ Taking baby steps
- ✓ Eating
- ✓ Exercising
- ✓ Taking my meds
- ✓ Staying sober
- ✓ Using my tools
- ✓ Talking about what's going on
- ✓ Letting myself be okay with not being okay
- ✓ Taking care of Nala
- ✓ Not giving up on myself.
- ✓ Trying
- ✓ Smiling

Overall, I know I will be okay, if I continue to take things one second at a time, one minute at a time, one hour at a time, one day at a time. Because at the end of the day, that is the only thing I can do. Tomorrow is not guaranteed, and just for today, I am in the present moment and working and getting stuff done that I wouldn't be able to do if I was still living my life in chaos and drinking. Dealing with trauma will come with time. Forgiving myself and others will come in time. Being physically healthy and financially secure will come in time. The only thing that will not come in time is if I give up on myself and hurt myself on a temporary feeling or emotion. I think that is the biggest thing that I am learning about myself. Feelings and emotions can't hurt me. What can hurt me is myself—physically, mentally, emotionally, and spiritually. If I continue to trust God and lean on him when things are tough, I can get through anything because the true purpose of living is living a life in relationship with God, which is what I am finally doing for the first time in my life, after living with the devil for thirty-one years.

DAY 5

Thursday, January 5, 2023

I woke up and started my day at 4:30 a.m. I got ready and packed up my laundry and met my dad at doggy day care, where Nala had her first assessment at a day care. It was hard leaving her, and yet I knew she was going to be great. I went to my parents' house and started my laundry and began working.

At noon, the day care called and said Nala passed her assessment and that she is welcome at any time. I was so happy for her and knew she would be great. I went through my day and noticed that my anxiety would spike every thirty minutes or so. I used my skills and made sure I ate breakfast, had less than a cup of coffee, breathed, and even meditated during lunch. I was able to focus on work and get through the workday with getting a lot of work done. I was proud of myself for getting through another day, another workday. I am so close to the weekend where I can relax and decompress from this very long week. The thing that I noticed the most is that I tend to ruminate a lot without realizing that I am doing it. I will be focusing on work, and I have twenty different thoughts running around my brain at the same time. Moving forward, I am going to ask myself the following questions:

- What was I just thinking?

- Is that thought true? What is the evidence for the thought, and is there any evidence against the thought?

- Is that thought helpful? Does it move me in the direction of the things that are important to me?

- Is there something else I could tell myself that would be both more true and more effective in moving me in the direction of my goals?

- How does it make me feel?

- What does it prompt me to do in comparison with the thought I wrote down?

Negative thought: I should die or hurt myself or drink.

- The thought is not true, and I don't have any evidence these are the things I want to do. The evidence against this thought is that I do not want to die. I very much so want to be alive and see what positive things are in store for me in the future. I have no plan to hurt myself, nor do I want to hurt myself. I cannot drink because I am an alcoholic, and if I take one drink, I will not be able to stop, and I am powerless over alcohol, and it has made my life unmanageable. I will lose all the progress I have made in the last three plus months.

- This thought is not helpful because it does not move me in the direction of the things that are important to me, such as being positive and being grateful for everything that I do have in my life, such as my reconnection with my family, friends, and Nala. I am also no longer able to be negative because so many positive things are happening in my life. I am no longer in a toxic abusive relationship. I completed a three-month rehab program, and I came home and am managing the culture shock of being home again, living alone, plus grief because Sheri was killed.

- I can tell myself that it is okay to not be okay. Life is not always rainbows and sunshine. Life is hard, and it is messy, and it is painful. I can give myself a break and be nicer to myself because I am going through a lot of change—physically, mentally, emotionally, and spiritually and even financially. I don't have to have all the answers today. I can allow myself time and space to grieve the loss of Sheri. I can give myself time to adjust to being home as it has only been three weeks. I can let go of my unrealistic expectations of where I think I should be because I have a lot of trauma and loss in my past that I need to work through. I can be nicer to myself and continue practicing self-care that will make me feel better about myself physically, mentally, and emotionally.

- These negative thoughts make me feel unloved, unwanted, undeserving, and unneeded. I know that these thoughts are not my reality. I know that the devil is trying to take me down and have me go back to my old ways, and here I am standing against my negative thoughts and doing OEA.

- These feelings prompt me to fight even harder for myself and my life. To continue working on SEEDS (Sleep, Eating, Exercise, Doctor prescribed medication, and Sobriety). I am moving past my past and working on forgiving myself for my past mistakes, and instead of looking at them as mistakes, I am changing the wording and calling them lessons. I have had a lot of lessons in my life that has brought me to the present moment of working from my parents' house, my dog being at doggy day care, eating healthy and getting back on a sleeping routine.

- Fuck off, devil, you don't live here anymore. I am a child of God, and he is not going to allow you to live rent free in my head anymore. Your eviction notice is way past the expiration date, and as of today, you are no longer welcome in my head. God gave me strength today and allowed me to focus on work and get through this workday. He allowed me to be strong and helped me to rid of these negative thoughts and emotions.

- God is good. I am saved. I am a child of God. I am loved. I am wanted and needed in this word. My time is not over, and God has a plan for me. He loves me unconditionally, and I trust him with all my heart and soul even if some days I don't feel like I do. I feel safe with him physically and emotionally. I am looking forward to seeing what my future brings. I am going to continue staying positive and looking at the bight things of life. Life is supposed to be enjoyed even through the pain that it brings. That is why there is love. Love is the secret ingredient to life that most people may not realize they have. Love for oneself and love for those around you. Love for the universe and love for family. Love for your pet and love for God. God is the key that holds all this love, and all you must do is surrender and give your will over to him, and everything else falls into place. Having God in your life is a gift and not a punishment, as much as our society would like us to think that. We always want to blame someone, anyone besides ourselves for the choices we have made. No one has a gun to our heads and tells us to do a certain thing or act a certain way. We chose that all on our own. That is what we call to call free will.

DAY 6 TO 8

Friday, January 6, 2023

I took a break over the weekend from writing because it was the weekend and I left my laptop at my parents' house. I wanted to get on here and catch up on my first weekend of the New Year. On Friday, I worked and got through the day, and then I went home and relaxed for the evening. On Saturday, I came to my parents' house, and my dad and I sat down and looked at my finances. They are not great, but they are not horrific to the point I can't come back from it. I did get overwhelmed when my mom started throwing ideas at me at what I should be doing. I know she came from a place of love. It just was not the right time because I am in a fragile state and am learning how to take care of my SEEDS again. So far, the sleep is the only thing that is throwing me for a loop. I am having a hard time staying asleep and waking up at a normal time. My body is not understanding the fact that it is safe. I am safe. I keep having to tell my body this, but it keeps ignoring me and freaking out all on its own. I had a panic attack on Saturday. I danced with Aunt Natalie to express myself and feel my emotions. Overall, I got through the weekend and even went to church on Sunday and cleaned and got the things that I wanted done. I just am being hard on myself because I want to be in a different spot then where I am right now. I am trying to refrain my thought patterns and use my wise mind instead of my emotional mind.

I hate feeling like this: I may feel weak right now, and this too shall pass.

I am too tired to work: I am feeling tired because I did not get a restful night of sleep and will focus on the task on hand.

I am fat: My weight is not where I would like to be, and I am changing my habits to replace them with healthy ones.

I am never going to be healthy: I may not feel healthy right now, and in the future, I will make better choices regarding my health.

I will never get over Michael: Any breakup is difficult and takes time to heal from the damage that is done.

Doing this exercise made me realize that I do not have positive thoughts in my head right now and my negative brain is out and about and trying to start issues, and it is not even 9:00 a.m. yet. I am too hard on myself for the simplest things, and majority of the things that I am hard on myself for are out of my control—such as the fact that Sheri was killed and died, the fact that I am an alcoholic, the fact that I am an addict, the fact that I was born in Russia to horrible parents who neglected me and didn't take care of me. I only have control over myself and my own thoughts and actions. So I am challenging myself with some goals for this week:

Let go of the past

1. Forget about the future
2. Stay in the present moment
3. SEEDS
4. Meetings
5. Socialize

If any of these goals get hard to accomplish reach in your toolbox and use the following tools:

- Grounding (five senses)
- Wise mind
- OEA
- Self-compassion
- Self-love

DAY 9 TO 11

Tuesday, January 11, 2023

Right now it is 9:16 a.m., and my anxiety is spiking for some reason. I am not exactly sure why. I had breakfast. I got ten hours of sleep. I am taking my meds, walking Nala, and staying sober. I think this is a med issue. I am taking too much, and it is influencing my body. I feel very tired right now. I am having a hard time concentrating, and all I want to do is sleep. I think I am depressed and anxious at the same time. I must work, and yet my body is fighting me to stay awake. I am trying to do OEA and push through the tiredness. The last two days were fine in the sense I could focus and stay on task, and today I am struggling more than the usual. The up and down is kicking my ass. No wonder why I am so tired. I can't stay regulated to save my life. One minute I am fine, and the next, I am not. I don't completely understand why this continues to happen, and yet I must keep pushing through and allowing my body to keep getting used to the new dose of medication that I am on. Just for today, I am going to do the following things:

- Have self-compassion for myself
- Allow my body to go through the waves
- Cry if needed
- Shower and wash my hair
- Let go of the past as much as possible
- Breathe
- Drink water

Katia Smith

- Eat healthy
- Rest when needed
- Go to Bible study
- Slow down

I have a lot on my mind right now, and yet the only thing I can focus on is lying down. If only I can close my eyes for twenty minutes that would help me feel regulated. It is 9:24 a.m., and I am going to go downstairs and talk to my dad about this and see what he recommends I do.

I just got back from a walk around the block twice. I am listening to music and feel like I got some of my anxiety and depression out into the world that it is not inside of me. I think I am also going to do a meeting while working and hope that will help me. I am just so tired. I must continue pushing through, and if going on a walk is the answer, so be it. I miss Sheri so much. The word feels empty without her. I know she is in heaven with Jesus and in a better place. I wish I could understand or know why it was her time to go. I know I don't get to know these answers, and just knowing that God's timing is better than anything that there is for me to know. I talked to my mom, and she said that I am going to learn how to do hard things and push through the hard times. I am not going to be able to be blind to reality anymore and know that denialville is no longer accepting me. I was dying in denialville. It has not been easy in realityvile, and yet nothing worth it is easy. God choose me to do hard things, and I am not going to let him down. He brought me into this country to be able to be successful, and whatever his plan is for me, then so be it. I am a child of God, and he knows what he has in store for me. I must learn to trust him and allow him to work in my life the way he only knows. He had his reasons for Sheri's life to end, and it is not for me to know or understand. It is my job to get up each day and continue fighting for the good fight of being a follower of Jesus, picking up my cross every day, and pushing through the hard days and be present on the good days.

DAY 12 TO 19

Thursday, January 19, 2023

I have not written in a few days because I had a lot going on and it's been a busy week. This past weekend I was busy almost every day. Friday was Rachel's birthday, and we had a blast with Book Club at her house and played the game left-right-center and danced and laughed.

On Sunday, January 15, 2023, I was baptized in front of my entire church. Natalie, Charlotte, Nora, and Olivia all showed up to support me. I thought I would feel differently after being baptized, but I don't. A little bit maybe. But I still have the same issues as before I went into the water. The only difference is that I am now able to say that I am fully a child of God and I am saved. I am starting off my journey with Jesus, and I am suddenly feeling like I am starting over. I feel like I am meeting Jesus for the first time, even though I have always known him my entire life. For the first time in my life, I am allowing myself to have a relationship with him. I don't know why, but it's scary. I think it's because God is intimidating to me. I don't want to disappoint him. I want to be able to please him and not let him down, and I think for the first time I am realizing that he loves me even if I let him down or make a mistake or fall. He is the kind of friend that will pick you up when you fall and walk with you and not point and laugh at you. So when I stood up there in front of everyone and allowed myself to be vulnerable in front of God and others, I knew that is exactly where I needed to be. I needed to get baptized to show myself that I do love God and I do want to have a relationship with him; and even if I have had to restart my relationship with him daily, at least at the end of the day, I know that I am choosing him day after day, month after month, year after year. He is the King of kings, and he is the only one that I want to have a relationship with. Through him, I will be able to have healthy relationships with my friends and family. Through him, I will be able to heal myself from the inside out. I am on a journey, and I need to be able to step outside of myself and see it from a different perspective. I am on a journey to the past and future daily, and the only place that I really want to be in is in the present moment. I want to be able to be at peace and content in my own skin. Home, love, family—that is all that I am searching for. One step at a time I will be able to find my way in this crazy place we call earth, and if I find those three things, I think I will be at peace in my life.

The thing is that, I have all those things already. I have parents; I have a sister and brother; and I have my created family with Father Eddie, Aunt Natalie, and my friends who are like my sisters: Charlotte, Rachel, Sarah, and Susan. I have love because God loves me. I know my family loves me. I have multiple homes: Eddie's, parents', Natalie's, Charlotte's, and my apartment. All these places feel like home to me, yet I feel lost and empty. I feel lost and empty because I don't have my *own* family, love, and home that I have created for myself. I know in time I will have these things if I continue to stay sober. I know it will be a lot of hard work. By staying stable mentally, emotionally, physically, and spiritually, if I want the next thirty plus years to look different, I must become different in every single way. I must do the following things:

- *Physically*: Take care of my body, which means lose weight and eat healthy on the regular.

- *Mentally*: Take my medications and continue to work with my therapist twice a week.

- *Emotionally*: Letting go of the past, changing my thought patterns, change my actions, and stay in the present moment.

- *Spiritually*: Worship, prayer, service, journal, go to church, not be afraid to being vulnerable with God.

I have a lot of work ahead of me for 2023, and yet I am up for the challenge for the first time in my life. I am ready to change and never go back to the Katia from previous years. I know I will mess up and fall, but if I continue to get up and take things one step at a time and take each day as if it is the only one I had left, then I will be okay. I will start healing, and I will be able to get to a place of radical self-love. My goal is to be able to look back on this year and see how I have grown and how I have changed. I must let go of my old thoughts and behaviors because they are no longer serving me. The past no longer serves me. That is why it is in the past. I have already lived through it, and there is nothing that I can do to change it no matter how badly I want my story to be different. This is God's plan for me. Who am I to challenge God's will? I am not that important. I am just one person trying to find her way in this place we call Earth. I may not know what my purpose is yet, and the beautiful part is that I have time to figure it out. So buckle up, Katia, you have a wild year of ups and downs ahead of you. I hope you find time to enjoy the little things as those are what memories are built on. Learn to say *no* to the things that don't serve you and *yes* to the new things that will be the adventures of this next year!

DAY 20 TO 26

Thursday, January 26, 2023

What is this teaching me?
Take another step.
Trust.
Self-acceptance.
Never mind what is at the end, just take another step.

Grief, loss, change, new beginnings, closing chapters, growing pains, anxiety, depression— all these things have been keeping me in the past and in the future all week long. I have been struggling staying in the present moment. I am currently at my parents' house and working. I woke up from a horrible nightmare this morning. I was at my sister's wedding, and I was drunk to the point of doing things I normally wouldn't do. This made me very dissociated this morning. I decided to go to Starbucks and worked, and Kathy from church came and joined me for a cup of coffee. We talked, and I shared my story with her, and once I was done and it was her turn to share, I realized I was about to have a panic attack. I called Dr. Gibbons and my dad. He told me to come over, and so I wrapped up my visit and got into my car and drove to my parents' house. I spoke with my mom about my mental health and emotional health. They don't seem to understand what that means to me. I feel like it is going to take time for us to get in a place of them to understand just how much stuff I am juggling inside my head. Right now I am listening to a live podcast on *Insight Timer* by Michael, who I have been listening to for the last month or so. I have enjoyed being able to listen to him because the way he explains things allows me to understand. I have realized I am in a lot of pain, mentally and emotionally. I am now aware of who I am and who I want to be. I am a person of depth that one may not see when looking at me. There are a lot of layers to me. I have realized that I need to *slow down* when I am moving fast. It is hard for me to slow down. I am not happy with my job. I need to be able to get to a place where I am happy with my job. I am no longer numbing out. I am not responding the same way that I used to. I no longer want to blame those around me or myself for my past. I need to have self-compassion and empathy for myself. I must realize that I am a human being. I am not a robot. I am a person, and I cannot save everything and everyone from everything. All I can do is take everything one minute at a time, one hour at a time, and one day at a time.

To stay in today, I must be able to see the day for what it is—a gift. I have another day on this earth, and that is a gift from God. He does not want me to see me struggling and not being able function or quitting my job because I am going through grief. I am seeing that Sheri meant to me more than I could ever imagine. I feel like I took her for granted and was not able to fully appreciate her because I was so selfish and self-centered. This is what I learned today from the podcast:

Spiritually pain: one with soul and spirit. *I need to trust God.*

Mentally: false condition of self. (I am broken). *I am enough.*

Emotional pain: being able to feel (blocked). *I am grieving.*

Past: ego reactions (addiction) (pain). *My addiction wants me to numb.*

I am not just my ego. *I am a kind, compassionate, loving person.*

Respond: consciously (being present) (not perfection). *I am perfectly imperfect.*

Pity: approval and praise. *I do not approval from my parents to love myself.*

Emotional addiction: healing, love, not in control. *I am allowed to feel my feelings.*

Mental: consciously (I am not good enough, I am not loved, I am not wanted, I am not needed, etc.) *I am a child of God.*

Outside validation: lack of self-esteem. *I am learning to love myself each day.*

Acceptance or rejections my life. *I accept the fact that I am alive.*

Free will choice :give my power away. *I am choosing to live.*

Actively thinking about something that the impact has on me.

Honest feeling: feelings are not facts, compassion relief

Emotions are not logical.

Thoughts and feelings: self-punishment.

Who am I going to be today?

Deliberate choice making

Critical or curious

Day 27 to 29

Saturday, January 28, 2023

Today has been an emotional day. The last two days have been emotional days. This week has been an emotional week. The last twenty-eight days have been emotional days. I learned that I tend to demand to be heard when really I just need someone to hear me and listen to where I am. What can I say that I haven't said yet? I have been breathing and living OEA since the news of Sheri passing away. It seems, besides SEEDS, that it is the only thing left I can do besides journaling and meditating that is physically working. Mentally telling myself *I can* instead of *I can't* has helped me get through the day. Emotionally, I had to break down and cry today. I am not in a good place mentally. I am exhausted from not being able to sleep. I am forcing myself to eat because I need fuel for my body. I am forcing myself to walk my dog because it's not her fault I am depressed. I am taking my meds as prescribed, and I am staying sober, and yet I do not feel good. I am depressed. I can't tell if I am depressed because of the shock of losing Sheri or if I am depressed because of my mental health. I keep trying to do self-care by even getting my nails done today, and that helped for a little bit. I even made a new friend. That helped. And then I went back into the same dark hole. I come out for little bit, and then I have nowhere else to go besides lie on that cold floor in my head because right now that is the only place that is comfortable for me. My friends are trying to plan for my birthday, and yet I can't even get through the next five minutes.

January 29, 2023

It is 3:30 a.m., and I woke up an hour ago. Nala needed to go outside and go to the bathroom, so I let her out and brought her back in. I am trying to go back to sleep, but I am having a hard time sleeping for the last three days now. I am physically exhausted. Mentally, I am not suicidal, and yet I can't seem to be feeling extremely depressed. I know that you can feel depressed without being suicidal and not everything leads to someone wanting to end their life when they are depressed. I want to be alive because I have a lot to live for, and yet I can't seem to even myself out and get to a place where I am stable mentally. I reached out to Dr. Gibbons, and hopefully, he will get back to me sooner than later. Emotionally, I am drained. I have no energy to express emotions anymore. I am starting to shut down and not want to talk to anyone about where I am emotionally because it's hard to comprehend being grateful for the sober life you have and all the great things and people in your life and yet also feel completely hopeless in the regards of your mental health. I want to get to a place where I don't have to be the happiest person in the world but at least get to a place where I am not so down. They say if you are depressed, there is something from your past that you have not accepted or dealt with. My entire life I feel is what I have not accepted.

- Being born to alcoholics in Russia, who criminally did not take care of me, and my birth father who molested me and violated my body.
- Being adopted and being a difficult child growing up because of what I went through in Russia.
- Growing up and battling my own battle with men, addictions, and mental health.
- Sheri passing away.
- The fact that I am an alcoholic.
- The fact that I tend to compare myself to others.
- That I am codependent.
- That I feel so alone in a room full of people and yet knowing that God is with me, so I am not alone.

- Not being able to sleep through the night.
- Being hungry and yet not being able to eat.
- Feeling like that six-year-old living in Russia during the winter.

Today I am grateful for the following:

- God
- Music
- Laptops
- Word document
- Nala
- My bed
- Fire on YouTube channel
- My apartment
- My friends
- My family
- A new begging
- A new sober life
- Sobriety
- Legacy
- Thirty-seven gardenia
- Food
- Water
- Coffee
- My church
- My pastors
- My creative side
- My ability to feel
- My ability to cry

Katia Smith

- My ability to speak
- My ability to express myself through writing
- My ability to let go and let God
- My ability to accept life on life's terms
- My ability to being vulnerable
- My ability to listen
- My ability to ground myself
- My ability to grow
- My ability to do hard things
- My ability to take care of myself
- My ability to know what is good for me
- My ability to never give up
- My ability to being humble
- My ability of being empathetic

FEBRUARY: DAY 1

February 1, 2023

Today I worked from my church. I woke up at 6:30 a.m. and started my day. I got out of bed after doing a meeting and went to work and had a 9:00 a.m. meeting. Work was okay. It was low key, but my energy level was up and down today. At one moment, I could concentrate, and at other times, it was harder. I had 1 panic attack around 3:00 p.m. that lasted an hour and a half. I spoke to my two pastors, and we decided to come up with a plan of how to proceed with my mental health. I meditated around 5:45 p.m. and was able to get off the couch. I am still feeling depressed, anxious, sad, angry, lonely, and tired. I ate a little bit, and I think I am ready to call it a day. I don't want to go home yet, and yet I know I need to. I need to sleep, and that is all I want to do—*sleep*. Sleep eight hours of uninterrupted sleep, without waking up or dreaming of negative things. If I could just get some sleep, maybe I will be able to think clearly. The following file cabinets have been flying wild for the last week or so, maybe up to a few months or years.

- Being born to alcoholics in Russia, who criminally did not take care of me, and my birth father who molested me and violated my body. (Anger: red)

- Being adopted and being a difficult child growing up because of what I went through in Russia. (Anger: red)

- Growing up and battling my own battle with men, addictions, and mental health. (Anger: red)

- Sheri passing away. (Sadness: blue)

- The fact that I am an alcoholic. (Disgust: green)
- The fact that I tend to compare myself to others. (Fear: purple)
- That I am codependent. (Mixed feelings: red, blue, green, purple)
- That I feel so alone in a room full of people and yet knowing that God is with me, so I am not alone. (Joy, sadness: red, blue)
- Not being able to sleep through the night. (Red, blue)
- Being hungry and yet not being able to eat. (Green)
- Feeling like that six-year-old living in Russia during the winter. (Mixed emotions)
- Having to possibly go to another program
- Not being "fixed"
- Not having it all together (Sad, angry)
- Not being stable (Sad)
- Having to ask for help (Awkward)

February: Day 3

Decisions

February 3, 2023

I am feeling extremely anxious today. I woke up three different times last night and around 4:00 a.m. I knew I was dreaming. I wrote down in my sleep notes that I was blocked and not sure why. Whatever I was thinking and dreaming had me blocked and unable to stay asleep. Today I am working at my church to finish off this workday. I am feeling nervous for therapy today. I know we have to have a difficult conversation. We need to come up with a plan for the weekend as well moving forward because my mental health has not been great. The biggest reason is because I am not sleeping through the night. I am starting to not want to eat again, and then I also have a lot going on through my mind. Here are some of the things that are running through my mind.

- I am exhausted (physically, mentally, emotionally, spiritually financially).
- I want to run away (Florida).
- What am I running from?
- I don't want to feel my feelings.
- I am not happy at my job.
- I am tired of faking it until I make it.
- I am tired of waking up.
- I am tired of thinking about Michael.
- I am tired of feeling the way I do every single day.

Katia Smith

- I want to let go of some of this anxiety and depression but can't find a way to release it.
- Yet I am grateful.
- I want to quit my job.
- I am unhappy in my life.
- This is not the right place for me.
- Staying in the present moment is difficult.
- I feel lonely.
- Hungry.
- Angry.
- Tired.

I don't want to give up on myself.

February: Day 7

February 7, 2023

Today was a hard day. I had therapy at my church, and since all the offices were taken, I worked in the lobby, which wasn't as bad as I thought it was going to be. I had my session downstairs in the kids' room, which was hard because we had to talk about me being a six-year-old in Russia as well as my abortion. Two very heavy topics. Topics that I rather sweep under the rug and not think about. I also had my one-on-one with my manger, and I did not get good feedback, which put me in a bad mood because it seems no matter how hard I try it is never good enough and I am beyond unhappy at this job. I know I need this job because right now I have 0$ in my bank account. I checked it today, and I was in the negative. *Greeeatttt.* Just add to the pile of shit that I am dealing with. I am beyond lonely and tired right now. I met with my pastor today, and I need to stop asking the question *why* and *what*. Maybe it is time that I move on with my life and get over my past and try to live in the present moment.

I am currently at my church right now, and I just finished work. I got a lot of work done today, and yet tomorrow is a new day, and I must do it all over again. For whatever reason, I do not want to go home. I want to curl up in a ball on this floor and cry. I might just have to do that because it has been a very difficult day. I am trying to stay positive, and yet my mind wants to stay in the negativity. I pray God to give me a good night sleep tonight after all the caffeine I pounded. I am trying to take the next step of packing up my things and driving somewhere, anywhere that isn't running away from this day and this body and this mind and this world. This world is soooo broken. I pray I will get to a place of acceptance, self-love, and self-worth. I don't have much else to say. I am going to pack up and see where God takes me.

New Week

Monday, February 13, 2023

I haven't written in a week. Last week was a rough week because I did not get great feedback from my manager, and that had me spiraling all week long until this weekend. This weekend I went to the beach. I needed it so badly. It was a vacation away from reality. I was able to clear my head and think for the first time all week. During the work week, I can't focus on much besides work because I am so afraid that I am going to get fired from my job, and if I don't have any income coming in, then I really am going to be in a bad place mentally. I value working. I just don't particularly care for my job, which is why I am going to start looking around for something better, even though I enjoy being remote. I am going to let God lead me through what needs to be done with this one, only because I have no idea what I want to do with my life.

As my birthday approaches in a week, I have decided that instead of fighting turning thirty-two, I am going to be embrace it. I can't change it. It is going to happen if I want it or not, and even though I am single and have no kids and no career, I do know that I am loved by God. He wants me to be at peace, and I know Sheri is with me, even though she may not physically be here with me. She wants me to be happy.

I am feeling very tired today, and I do not like that because I wish I had more energy. I am always blah, and that bothers me because life is so short, and I wish to be happier and filled with joy. My cup has so many holes in it. I am constantly spilling out, and fixing the cup seems like a waste of time, and why don't I just get a whole new cup that will not be filled with holes? I should be ecstatic about the weather and what a beautiful day it is; and yet I haven't showered today, brushed my teeth, or even put on deodorant, let alone comb my hair. I guess today is another day of having a lot of spoons. I have three more hours of work. I think I am going to close my eyes for a little bit, and if I fall asleep, so be it. I can't force my body to stay awake. It's not fair to me to try to force myself. Today is a hard day. Sheri passed away today two months ago around this time, and it's about 1:00 p.m., and that is also a reminder that I have been home two months and going on five months of sobriety.

How—and I mean, *how*—have I not had a drink in the last two months? I feel like every day I am pushing by and unable to pick up that drink.

I know how. I am working the steps and talking to my sponsor daily and going to meetings. I may not be perfect at it, but I am working hard, and each day that goes by means that I am getting a little but stronger. I am getting paid soon, and taxes will get done, and before I know it, I will be back on my feet, and who knows, maybe I will learn how to save money moving forward since I am not drinking anymore. I no longer want to waste my life drinking and feeling sorry for myself. I have shit to do, and I don't have time to lie around. That can be done when I am dead. That sounds a tad harsh, but it's so true.

Katia Smith

Fired, Let Go

Wednesday, February 15, 2023

Today at twelve thirty, I was let go from my job at Trace3. I got fired. I was let go. Is there a difference? No. Dad and Mom said that I have an opportunity, and I am trying to take it step by step and see that even though a door has closed, it doesn't mean another one will not open. I am feeling sad, disappointed, confused, vulnerable, and completely devasted that this has happened. I told myself years ago that I was never going to be fired from a job again. And yet here I am. I know I should not be using the word *fired* as it is negative and makes the whole situation worse, and yet I can't help but feel a certain way about how Trace3 and Nicole handled it. I feel like under the circumstances that I was in, I don't know if I was really treated in the best way. Does it really matter how I was treated? I have to accept that I am no longer at Trace3 and that my new full job is to look for a new job. My anxiety is high right now. I am trying to breathe through it and get what I need done. My emotions are trying to get the best of me, and I refuse to allow them because I am one day away from being five months sober. One day and yet that is all it takes—one day for all my shit to blow up in my face. I keep thinking that this is temporary and it too shall pass, and yet I can't seem to catch a break. I have to take care of myself, and then I am trying to do that. So I am going to continue with SEEDS to the best of my ability.

UGHHH…

AHHH…

AHHH…

FUCKKK…

SHITTT…

WTF!

I FUCKING HATE THIS!

I HATE THIS SO FUCKING MUCH!

WHY ME!

WHY! WHAT! WHO! WHAT IS GOING ON!

I HATE LIFE! HATE IT WITH A PASSION!

I WANNA DRINK!

AND SAY FUCK IT!

FUCK ALLL OF THIS!

Don't cry, Katia.

Don't cry, Katia.

Don't cry, Katia.

Don't cry, Katia.

Don't cry, Katia.

Don't cry, Katia.

Don't cry, Katia.

Don't cry, Katia.

Don't cry, Katia.

Don't cry, Katia.

Don't cry Katia.

Last Day of a Very Long Month

February 28, 2023

Well, its officially the last day of February. My birthday came and went, and it was amazing. I was surrounded by love and friends and family. I was able to stay sober during it, and even ended up at the beach with Charlotte. I am trying to hold on to that feeling of pure happiness, and I know it isn't realistic to always be happy, and yet all I want is to stay in that moment when life didn't seem so scary. And yet as the days go by and I get closer to what I need to do, it seems like it just will not end. The dread and despair seem to follow me even when I am asleep, and I can't shake it off me no matter what medications I try, how much I meditate or walk or eat or sleep. It is a part of me, like the curse that I was born into. I know I am talking really negative right now, so I am going to catch myself in this moment and refrain the thought and write about the birthday card that Charlotte got for me. It says:

> Where friends are...
> Smiles are generous.
> Kindness is multiplied.
> Sorrows are softened.
> Laughter is healing.
> Years are celebrated.

On the inside, Charlotte wrote:

Dear Katia,

When you have a friend who makes you laugh and very often makes your day…you know what joy is. When you have a friend who is a good person with a gracious heart and gorgeous spirit…you know what peace is. When you have a friend whose beauty (inside and out) is matched only by her compassion for others… you know what love is. Because I have you for my best friend, I kno2w what it is to be truly blessed! <3

With much love on your birthday-
Charlotte
Xoxo

These words have stuck with me ever since I got this card. The way she views me is the complete opposite of what I thought I was, and yet as I read, I can see that she is right. I do have a compassionate heart, good spirit, and beauty inside and out. I have seen videos of that happy girl, and she is in me waiting to be let out, and I am the only one that has the key to let her shine. I am terrified regarding the job thing. It has been a blow to my ego and confidence, and I know in time and hard work, I will find something better and God will provide for me like he always has and will, and when the time comes, I will be able to support myself in more than one way. I physically need to start taking care of my body. As the weather gets nicer, I am going to continue taking Nala on longer walks and going to the dog park and maybe start making smoothies. I want to be mentally heathier by taking care of my triggers and thoughts and emotions and not live in emotion mind all the time. Emotionally, I want to continue feeling my emotions and not numbing them out with drugs or wine. Staying sober has been such a wonderful gift for myself. If I cannot drink over Sheri's death or losing my job, I can do it all. Spiritually, I continue trusting God.

Faith over Fear

False Evidence Appearing Real

Monday, March 20, 2023

I haven't written in a while because I have been in a depression state, which has been having me sleeping a lot and struggling getting out of bed. I have also not been sleeping well. I keep having nightmares, and I think it's because of my PTSD and anxiety. I never thought that I would end up being someone who struggles with sleep.

It's a new day, and it's almost 2:00 p.m., and I have a to-do list that is so long that it overwhelms me. I know when I am depressed, I let myself and those things around me go. I am trying to get better, but some things are out of my control. Acceptance of things I cannot control is a struggle that I have had my entire life. I have always wanted to be in control because there have been so many situations in my life where I have felt out of control. I am six months sober, and the last three months of being home has been a challenge for me because I forgot what it feels like to be able to take care of myself every single day. I keep thinking about what my therapist wants me to do. I think writing a letter to the six-year-old me is difficult because I don't remember much and yet feel as if I do. From what I do remember it was not pleasant.

Today I am grateful for the following things:

- Breath in my lungs
- Candles
- Nala

- A bed
- Roof over my head
- The ability to feel
- My nails
- Food
- Freedom

I think freedom is a huge one for me. I have a feeling that because I am no longer with Michael, I am constantly wondering when I will have my freedom taken from me again. He took so much from me. He took my heart and didn't give it back to me, and now I have to live with a shattered heart and hope that the glue will keep it together. I am constantly feeling despair. I am trying to change that to having faith. If I have faith in God and trust that he will take care of me and heal me from the inside out, then I will be able to get to a place of acceptance of myself and all the layers that make up me. I will not look at the past and cringe. I will not live in the future and worry all the time. I can be in the present moment. Being in the present moment gives me the ability to feel peace, which is what God has always been trying to give me, I think.

I don't know if I need to apologize to you, God, but I feel like I need to because I have been blaming you for the death of Sheri. It is still hard for me to wrap my head around it.

REHAB 2.0

July 29, 2023

I am currently lying in bed back in New Jersey at rehab. I am having a hard night because I do not feel like I know what I am doing anymore. I relapsed on pot again. Which means, I lost my fucking mind. I am trying to stay positive, and yet it is easier said than done. I am still physically exhausted, and mentally and emotionally, I am broken. Spiritually, I am holding on by a thread.

God, if you can hear me, please hear my prayer. I cannot go through this again. I am feeling like I am broken. I am so tired of dealing with all this shit. I want to have a happy and healthy life. I do not know what else to say besides what I have said. I am struggling so fucking bad right now. I want to run away and never come back home and let everyone move on with their lives.

July 30, 2023

I woke up feeling better than I did yesterday. I know I am going to have my good days and my bad. I am going to meet with Madison, who I asked to be my sponsor while I am here at Legacy. I met with Madison and then I started step work.

Job Searching

September 9, 2023

I am currently at Natalie's house applying for jobs while waiting for her workers to get here. I am feeling overwhelmed because it is stressful applying for jobs and not getting any responses. I am staying motivated because I can't rely on my church to pay for my bills anymore. I have a few weeks left to go before I get to be completely broke. This has become very difficult very fast. I am trying to stay positive and keep on putting in applications, and yet all I want to do is scream on top of my lungs. I hate America sometimes, because this whole concept of money and having a job is overrated. Whoever decided that this is how we must live really was a fucking douche bag.

I know all of this is based on fear, and I will be able to find something sooner than later. If I keep on applying and putting myself out there, then something has to fall through. The thing that I don't understand is they say they want to hire someone and yet they have no fucking clue how to respond when someone applies for the position. *I just want a fucking job!*

Sex

Thursday, September 21, 2023

Last night I had sex with Mikey from Bumble, and I am kind of regretting it, because I wish that I didn't lead with my vagina and instead listen to my mind and those of Natalie, Charlotte, and Sarah because they told me not to have him over. But instead of listening to them, I did what I wanted to do, and I am realizing that he is a tad odd and off, and now I have another number of how many men I have slept with, and it is not something that I am proud of. I am not comfortable in my own skin, and yet I am sleeping around with men that I don't know because I am trying to prove to myself that I am over Michael and he has not effect on me, and that is not true. I don't feel comfortable.

My sister made a comment to me yesterday that she thinks that I am a lesbian, and I was insulted by it. I thought it was rude of her to make such a comment, especially since she knows that it is not true. I know that by me sleeping around, I am not going to find a man that is going to want to stick around with me. I should start listening to my girlfriends about how to interact with men, because *steps over pets*, right? I am not even following my own rule when it comes to dating and sleeping around. I don't feel comfortable in my own skin, and because I don't like the way I look, I am looking to have someone boost my ego by having someone be attracted to me sexually. I am trying to have self-compassion toward myself. I know that I am not perfect, and maybe I am not ready to date.

I always wonder why those around me have what I want. I wonder when and how am I going to meet the person I am supposed to be with.

I don't think I am going to. I truly have a fear that I am going to end up alone for the rest of my life and never find the love that I think I deserve because I don't think I have much to offer and those who are out there are not going to want me because I am fat. I really wish I wasn't as big as I am. What can I do to lose the weight that I am currently carrying around. I can do it like Mikey and just not eat for a few days and just drink water to stay alive, and yet that is not the healthy way to do it. Being positive has been hard the last few days because I am not working and have no money and am fat. How is that so? What do I have to offer?

Onto the next. Now I have to figure out how to let him down easily, and maybe I will meet someone new that is more my type.

WEED

October 11, 2023

Today I was driving home, and I realized that I could see the vape that I threw out my car lying right there on the street, so I parked my car and went to the street and picked it up and brushed it off and took a hit that was around 2:00 p.m. Since then, I have been smoking and driving and was gone all day. I went to church today to help with cleaning up the sanctuary, and I got on my hands and knees and prayed the serenity prayer repeatedly. I then left church and went to Natalie's house where we talked for hours about different topics. We ate together and talked about family and the difference between friendships and family and how we have different versions of ourselves.

All I wanted to say to her was that I was not sober. I relapsed again on weed, and I was sober for three days. But the words and the tears couldn't come out, probably because it was freezing in her house since she doesn't have any heat until Friday. Anyways, I am currently lying in bed, and it is almost 9:00 p.m. I have my calming rain and fireplace in the background. I am lying in my bed that feels very warm. Nala is barking and has finally settled down and is now on the bed. My heart is racing, my thoughts are racing. TIPP, five senses. I really want to call Noah right now. I filled out the call sheet, and that was intense, and so I took another hit of the pen. And now I know I am high because I am coughing. I am feeling everything and nothing at the same time. I feel all the pain, and yet I fell nothing. I feel all the emotions, and yet I feel nothing.

WHO IS GOD?

God is sovereign, God provides, God is holy, God is love, God is safe, God is trustworthy, God is always present, God is kind, God is fair, God is friendly, and he is comforting. God is emotionally available, and he is a thought away. God is forgiving, and he is patient. He does not judge, and he does not condemn. He is understanding, and he is positive. He provides, and he is willing. He is a good listener, and he never complains. God is infinite, and he is everywhere at any given moment. He is unchangeably compassionate and wise. He is gracious and beautiful. He is accepting and welcoming and encouraging. God is God, and I am not God. I am a creation of God in his image, and his will is the only will that I want to live by.

DEAR SHERI

October 19, 2023

Sheri,

It has been ten months, six days, and countless hours since you passed away. I am currently lying in my bed in my bedroom with Nala in the bed with me. It's 9:34 p.m. My sponsor and therapist both think I need to write you a letter to express how I am feeling. I think it's bullshit that all I have left of you are lyrics of songs that remind me of you, and I am afraid that I am losing the part of me that remembered you because all I have left are photos. That reminds me of your brown hair, beautiful eyes, and a smile that lit up every room it ever walked into. In time, I will not start healing, because what you did was so awful that I am afraid that one day I will end up like you. Because I know the feelings of depression, and trauma, and abandonment, I know the feelings of having a fucked-up family. I know the feeling of feeling alone and feeling like no matter how many people are around me that feeling of loneliness, that sadness never really goes away. Do you know what I thought tonight? What if Nala and I just walked out into traffic, would it really hurt? Well, guess what, Sheri? Book Club, Eddie, my family, my friends, and God came into my mind. So I am not going to pretend to know what you were going through or feeling because whatever it was it was valid. Because at the end of the day, you were human, and you had emotions. You felt fear, sadness, and anger; and you also felt joy, and happiness, and love. Idk if you can see me, feel me, or remember me; but I remember you. I remember the way you were a mother to me. You welcomed me into your home, into your family and treated me like one of your own. I don't know if I have ever expressed that to you. That is how you made me feel. So safe. I had never felt safe like I did walking into your house and being greeted with the biggest hug and kiss, with Paulie demanding kisses and attention. Depending on what was going on, we would either share a meal together as a family or catch up quickly before running off to the next thing. Sheri, I am mad. No, I am angry. I am so fucking angry that I could burst from the inside out. I am crying right now because I am in so much pain from this decision that you made. I don't fault you. I know you must have been in pain. So much pain that only God could take it away. And damn it, I am jealous of God for having you. So here I am on a Thursday night lying in bed writing you a letter. A *letter*! I can't call you. I can't text you. I can't hug you. I can't kiss you. I can't do anything anymore but remember you. I know you are in heaven, because the God that I believe in is kind, and loving, and caring, and welcoming, and knew your spirit. And your spirit will never fade from the face of the world because in the world is your face, everywhere, because we are still alive. We can talk about you, we can share, we can laugh, we can cry, and, dammit, we can be angry. That is what It means to be human. *To feel*. I can feel so many things at once—anxiety, depression, flashbacks, BPD, addiction, trauma, shame and guilt. And that's okay. I don't want to be angry at you. It doesn't feel right, like I am shameful for feeling an emotion. That is why I think I am full of fear, and that is why I do not like feeling anger. Yet I am also filled with sadness and happiness. I am so grateful I have a book club, babies on the way from Charlotte and my sister, and yet I can still feel the pain of losing my own child due to abortion. You were there for me. I called you, desperate and in pain because I had no one. In that moment, I had nothing. And you came, and you picked me up and took me to your home where you took care of me while going through your own pain regarding you son that I had no idea about until the night Eddie came to Natalie's and told me. I didn't know that about you. I feel like there is a lot I didn't know about you. I am starting to feel a lot of anger right now as I am writing this. I am breathing, I am typing, I am alive. I am breathing, I am typing, I am alive. I am alive, and you are not. Yet I believe, Sheri. I believe that I will see you again. This can't be the end. Book Club is not done, and it will never be complete until we are all together again as one. As much as we love Eddie, which we do with all our hearts, and man, he is strong Sheri. Idk how he stands. I would be in a hole somewhere, LOL. He is not *you*! *You is who we want. You are the one that keeps us up at night. You are the one that has broken our hearts. You are the one that abandoned us. You are the one that said she loved us and left. We didn't do anything to deserve this. We deserve better than this, because at the end of the day God is love. And love is not what took you. What took you was something that one should not speak of. Because I know God had you in that moment, in that final moment before you crossed over to the other side. Where you are, close and near. Where you are, in the bedroom in my heart. That is where you live now. But mostly in my* gut *because there are too many feelings in my heart and my brain is a liar. So I am going to bless you and going to change me because that is all I can do. I can't live angry. I have to give it to God. God knows what to do, and I don't.*

I don't know what I am doing anymore, God. I am so lost. I need guidance. I am dying. I am thirsty. I am in need. I am asking please take this from me. May thy will be done. This is a big one, God, but please take our Sheri and keep her close by and introduce her to Shannon and Megan. I would really hope that she gets to be with Dominick again, and that she is getting the chance to love my child, because no matter where she is at the end of the day, she will always be my mother.

SISTER

What can I say about my sister? There is so much that comes to my mind, and at the same time I feel like I can't say half the things I would like to because they are not nice, and who am I to not speak nicely of someone, especially my sister and the mother of my soon-to-be niece, Emma. I love my sister with all my heart, and I always will. She was with me since I was born, and she took care of me in Russia. She was the only one that had my back and watched over me while we were on the streets and in the orphanage. She kept me from harm daily, and she was only eight years old. That is a lot of pressure to put on a child, and yet I too was only a child. Trying to navigate through abandonment, hunger, and dying of pinworms because we had to eat out of the garages. Look at us two children were up against, and yet we survived. We got adopted and came to America. We got a second chance at life, and I had an emergency appendicitis to remove the pinworms and lived to talk about it. Yes, we were blessed.

We were alive, and we had parents that were placing a roof over our head and food in our belly for the first time in our lives. We were safe—physically, mentally, and emotionally. I believe my sister had to turn everything from Russia off because it was too hard for her to process it. I, on the other hand, had to open that can of worms and navigate through the trauma and learn how to heal from it, which I am still doing to this day. From this point on, I believe this is when we truly always were two different people, and that is okay. She is amazing, and strong, and resilient; and yet so am I. I have lived to tell stories that others would have a hard time believing.

I am trying not to get emotional because I don't know if I can handle everything that I am feeling right now. I am angry, sad, disappointed, and abandoned, and lastly, I am lonely. I feel very alone in these emotions. Every single day. Yes, everyone has emotions, and we all feel all these daily, and yet this is not about what everyone feels. This is about how I am feeling toward my sister, and right now I am truly sad that this is where we are in our relationship. How did we go from being bonded through abandonment to being complete strangers. So here I go. I am going to share how I truly feel about my sister up to this point, and it will not be easy to say, and at the same time, I know it will be healthy for me to get all of this off my chest so that I can let go of the expectations I have for my sister and accept her for where she is right now in her life. I can bless her and change me.

I am currently not working, and I am reminded of this almost daily through those that care most about me and, oh yeah, also from my anxiety and depression that is showing daily, because the stress of not having a job is not only in my body, but also in my mind. I am so stressed out about not having a job that I took out a withdrawal from my 401k and am using that money to pay off credit cards and other debt that I have not being able to do because I have no money. I also went grocery shopping for the first time in months last night, and that was so stressful, not only because of the money but also because I was around people again. All the sensations running through my body and seeing and moving around people was enough to give me an anxiety attack. I was able to get through it and get home and unpack the groceries.

When I woke up this morning, I was able to stay awake and not go back to bed even through my body was screaming at me to just close my eyes and shut out the world. I fought through that. By the time, it was 9:30 a.m. I had gotten out of bed, walked Nala, gotten some coffee, and did something on my laptop. And then I started saying good morning to those that I care about, and my sister is one of those people. I care about her, and I want her in my life and especially now that she is pregnant with her first child, and I will be an aunt. I love my sister. I do. She is my only blood. She is the only thing in this world that took care of me. And now that we are adults, I am trying to learn how to take care of myself, and I will always need my sister, and yet I don't know if I always can trust my sister with where and who I am because of the way she responds when I try to set a boundary with her or express how she makes me feel. My emotions are not safe with my sister. She gets defensive and mean and passively aggressive.

I get scared, quiet, standoffish, and retreat. That is where I feel safe. When I am talking to my sister, or anyone from my family, I am unable to stand up for myself because I am afraid of them. I am afraid of disappointing them, hurting their feelings, and lastly, I am afraid of making them angry. When they get angry, they are mean and hurtful and shut the door in my face and act as if I don't exist. They would tell me I am being overdramatic; that I am sensitive, emotional, and wrong. And all I want to say to them is "I don't need you to fix it for me or give me suggestions. What I really need is for you to listen to me and try and understand my feelings. I'm looking for you to be there for me. Do you think you could do that for me?" So that is what I did. That is what I said, and I don't know how she will respond, but all that I know is that I said what I was feeling, and no one is ever going to make me feel like I don't have a voice and that I don't matter because I do. I am not going to give in to their bullying and aggressive communication. I was trained for this through all my therapy. I was trained in how to regulate my own body and how to use a wise mind to challenge thoughts and assertive communication to express how I am feeling. I have these tools in my toolbox, plus meditation, music, journaling, and willingness to change.

So here we go. Let's embrace the future and say "Fuck you" to the past. Let's live in the present moment. I love you, Emma. You are my sister. I look up to you. I respect you. I am jealous of you at times. With that being said, I feel like you do not know who I am. We have not seen each other in years, and I am going to be direct with you. I am still hurt over the fact that you did not invite me to your wedding and kicked me out because of my choice to be with Michael. I know you feel that I chose him over the family, and that is valid. The truth is, that is not, and never has been, true. I was stuck. I was stuck in a cycle of domestic violence. I know this may sound like an excuse to you, and yet I need you to hear me when I say that I wouldn't call it that unless that was the truth. I know you have never been in a relationship with domestic violence, and you may not understand. That is okay. I don't need you to understand; I just need you to listen to me and respect my past. Just like I must respect the fact that you did not want me at your wedding because of the choices I made regarding Michael. You did what was best for you, and I did what was best for me. We may not agree on this, and it is still a fact.

So with that, I would like to move forward in our relationship. I would like to start fresh and let go of the past and not ruminate on it anymore. So to be able to do this, I need your help. If you can move forward and respect my boundaries and see that I am trying to change my life for the better. I may be moving at a slower pace than those around me, and it doesn't look like a route you would take. I just want you to know that I am healing. Every day. We all are. Can't wait to see you when you move back. It's going to be interesting.

Clearly, my sister is always going to be my sister. And at the end of the day, she is carrying my niece in her belly, which at the end of the day is her child. So whatever happens will happen. I pray that I will be a part of my niece's life and she knows how much she is loved already. So in my opinion, you got all the good shit, and I got all the consequences. But what you don't know about me is how many times I have risen from the ashes, how many times I have broken down and gotten back up. That is something that you may not understand, but don't worry, you don't have too. Because I am going to show you my actions, and from there, you will be able to see that I am who I am, and I do not apologize. This is how God made me, and I am exactly where I am supposed to be, and if you can't see that, then keep on looking because I don't have the time or the energy to be your punching bag. I am not the same Katia from five to six years ago, and you are not the same person that I use to call my sister. I will always love you, but for right now, I don't like you very much.

BEACH DAY

Tuesday, October 24, 2023

It is an eighty-degree day in Chicago in October, and I had to be part of it. I decided to take Nala and me to the beach. We went and played. I just got out of the shower, and I am so proud of myself that took a huge weight off my shoulders. I am feeling more relaxed now that I showered off the last few days. My throat is still hurting, and I am trying to not focus on it. Even on days like today, I can see that I am not having a good day mentally, and I can see that I am struggling mentally and emotionally. Today is Wednesday October 25, 2023, and I am currently at my church, in the living room, waiting to have a conversation with my pastor, and then right after that, I have therapy at 3:00 p.m., and I am going to have to talk to Noah about the way that I am and have been feeling for the last week. The last time we talked, it was about anger, and I wrote a letter to Sheri, expressing my anger, and even went and read it to her, and yet I don't know what I thought that was going to do. I ran away because I was afraid she was going to judge me and she died. I am afraid of the dead judging me. My whole life has been based around fear and not faith. I have been so afraid of living that instead I have been dying slowly.

I don't want to do this anymore. I want to be able to live my life the way I want to live it and not have judgements or criticism, and yet I know that is not reality, and I have to radically accept the fact that those that I care about and those that care about me are going to have an opinion on how I live my life. Those that are there to support me through it are the ones that are really my family—that is, my book club: Charlotte, Natalie,

Sarah, Rachel, and Susan. *They* and my pastors and the friends I have made along the way and have stood by me are my family.

My sister will always be my blood, and I pray that we will be able to learn how to live in this world where we do not see eye to eye. For the sake of her unborn child, I hope I can be a part of her life. I hope I can see her grow up and show her that having emotions is not a bad thing; it is a beautiful thing.

I am not sorry for who I am, and yet I am sorry for the things that I have done. I am sorry for the people that I have hurt along the way. Those who tried to help me. Those who listened to me endlessly. I am proud of the person that I am today. I have worked my ass off to get to where I am today. I have battled so many battles and overcome a *war* within myself, within my relationship with God.

NEW JOB

Thursday, October 26, 2023

I am officially sober. I threw the THC vape out of my window while I was driving home last night, and I have not used it since—obviously, since it was thrown out the window. What I mean is that, I am overall feeling exhausted because I have been trying to stay awake for Bumble Mike the last two nights, and he has not shown up like he says he will, so I am done. I am trying to not care about him as much as I think I do because who I really care about is Adam, and he is not in any shape to see me. I miss him. I miss seeing him and sleeping next to him. Let's be real, I miss any man that I can sleep next to.

I am trying to focus on the present moment, and right now I am getting my car fixed. All I need is an oil change, but every time I come into this place, they find something wrong with it. I don't understand how much more money I can put into this car. I haven't even paid if it off yet, and I feel like all my money either goes to rent or this car or bills. I have no time for myself and doing something nice for myself. I guess maybe this is why I took the money out of my 401k. It is to be able to get ahead of myself with bills and such.

Things I need to pay for:

My car = $12,094.61

Rent = $1,600

Misc. Bills = $500

FEELINGS

November 1, 2023

I am currently lying in bed, and it is 11:23 a.m. on Wednesday, November 1, 2023. Scott just left a little bit ago. He came over last night for sex, and that is my doing. I keep inviting him and Adam over to my apartment to have sex with me because I am lonely and I don't want to think or feel what it is that I am feeling—grief, sadness, depression, anxiety, and being misunderstood. I see my sister and Charlotte moving on in their lives without me, and even though I might be there physically in person mentally and emotionally, I am pulling away because I can't think of the possibility that something might go wrong, and then things will never be the same. I love my sister, I do. She is my only blood in this entire world that I know of. And yet I am so hurt by our last interaction. She said a lot of different things, but the one thing that I picked up is that she doesn't really want me in her life. She has everything she needs: a husband, baby on the way, parents who are helping her, and then there is me—the person who can't get it together; who is mentally unstable and emotionally wrecked daily; has BPD, grief, trauma, PTSD; who is constantly in therapy and going to rehab and getting involved in a domestic violent relationship. Those are the choices I've made in the last five to six years. That is what I've been dealing with for the last five to six years—*life*. So if this is not growing up, I don't know what is. I am the one that has been walking around on eggshells around the Smith family and everyone that is involved on the Hogan side and the Smith side. Everyone that has been around the last five to six years is living their own lives. Not many people from the family have seen me lately, and yet I am going to see them in a few weeks. But do you know who is in my life? Book club, Liam, Charlotte, and those I choose to call family.

I am having an overwhelming feeling as I am writing this. I am not used to saying what I think or feel. I am texting with Liam right now, and he is saying that I am not these things. I may struggle with mental health and going through grief, but at the end of the day, I am not these things. They are a part of me, and I struggle daily with these things. That is why I make sure that I sleep, eat, exercise, take my meds. and stay spiritually fit.

I am currently feeling like I am having a panic attack because I am writing about things that are difficult for me to talk about. It is hard for me to have self-compassion for myself and know that I am not alone in this world with these thoughts, emotions, and urges. I don't know what to do anymore. I am so alone and lost mentally and emotionally. I can sit here and pour out my guts time and time again, and yet it gets me nowhere. I keep doing the same thing repeatedly and expecting a different result. Today is a new day. Today is Natalie's birthday. Today is a day of celebration. Today is a day of happiness and joy and laughter. Today will not be a sad day because I don't have time to be sad. I mean, I do, but there is a time and place for it.

Thoughts Aren't Real, Thoughts Are Not Facts: Mindful

Thursday, November 2, 2023

I am lying in bed listening to music, and I can see Nala sleeping. I can touch my keyboard, and I can taste coffee. I am feeling sad, anxious, depressed, and lonely. And yet I am also feeling contentment as I lay in bed with a nice cup of coffee with candles on and music playing in the background. I am taking the time to do self-care and journal about what I am thinking and feeling so that I can maybe one day help someone. I am a child of God. I am a human who is flawed, and I wake up every day flawed, and yet that doesn't stop me from getting out of bed and brushing my teeth and taking my meds and doing something with this thing we call life.

I have this friend, and his name is Liam. I have known him since I was in high school. He was friends with my sister, and I would always want to hang out with them because I thought they were so cool, and as time went on, life took us in separate directions. But then Liam reappeared in my life. I don't remember what day or year or month it was. It was as if God knew that I needed him back in my life because I needed a friend that I could rely on and depend on to be honest with me every single day. And that is what he does. He cares about my well-being—physically, mentally, emotionally, and probably even spiritually. I feel safe with him. I can trust him. I can have emotionally intimate conversations, and yes, we have had a little physical contact. Sue me. I am a woman of needs. LOL.

But the needs that I need are not the same as others because I am not them. I am me. And that is just enough because God created me in his image, and he loves me unconditionally because I am who I am. That is how God loves. That is the love that I believe in. The love that no one on this planet can give me and that I don't want it from. I want that love for God. I need it because without him, I am so lost it isn't even funny. And yet we are the ones that run away, because we get scared. And I am using the word *we* because as a community on this planet earth *we* are of one, and that one is of God. He created us to be brothers and sisters and to love each other despite how we may feel regarding one's race, religion, and political stand. While these things are important, on a deeper level, they will never matter because God does not see race, religion, and political stand. He sees your soul.

If you allow him in, he can see it every day of each day that you are on this earth. So when it comes time to go, it isn't as scary because you know you have God and all your loved ones on the other side waiting for you. If you sit still calmly and take a deep breath in and let it out, you can see the present moment in front of you. If you calm your mind and open yourself up and pray this simple prayer of, "Lord, here I am," see what happens.

Close your eyes.
Listen.
Feel.
Cry.
Breathe.

And then keep on carrying on because time does not stop and life will pass you by. Having emotions is not the end. It could very much be the beginning of something truly exciting and special.

As I took the time to pray and answer a phone call, I realized that I am feeling a lot of different emotions right now and I am using my skills to get through each moment, minute, hour, and day. That is what my superhero power is. I survive. I get up, and I suit up, and I survive another day. This is what my role and purpose is on this planet. To love and accept myself for who I am inside and out and to love God unconditionally, because he loves me unconditionally.

CURRENT MOMENT

Wednesday November 8, 2023

I am currently texting between Steve and Scott, and man, I tell you, these men are so hungry for sexual things. They are just as horny as I am, and I am totally digging it. The only thing I need to figure out is which one is the one that will show up tonight, and if they show up tonight will I be pleased with what I have received? I am still enjoying my Christmas decorations and my fake fire that I have playing in the background as I sit on the couch this Wednesday night at 8:31 p.m. I have so much on my mind, so I am going to bulletin point them to make this all come out faster.

- Emma: moved back from Florida, currently fifteen minutes away from me—trigger
- Michael: getting rid of his stuff, has risen safety issues (internally mostly)—*huge trigger*
- Meds: are they helping or hurting me?
- THC use; is this hurting me or helping me?
- Panic: using coping skills to get through each moment
- Sheri
- Holidays
- Thanksgiving
- Christmas
- Charlotte's baby shower
- Life

- Feeling sadness and loneliness
- Sheri
- Michael
- Liam
- Scott
- Steve
- Adam

Thoughts:

What am I doing?
Am I okay?
Do I need to call someone?

Inside Out

Thursday, November 9, 2023

I am currently high lying in bed at 10:24 p.m. I have had yet another long day full of ups and downs. I just went online and chose a publisher, and I have no idea what I just got myself into because if this gets published, a lot of things are going to be out there in the world. And yet maybe, just maybe, for once this can be just for me and no one else. Maybe, just maybe, I can have one win in my life. Maybe I can stop pretending to be perfect, and just maybe I could be a human for just one day. Everyday feels the same. The one thing that is different are the variables that play in different scenes.

Today was a long and eventful day. I woke up at 11:00 a.m., and my leg was hurting, and I decided to go to Sarah's. I helped her with some steaming, and after getting our jimmy johns, I headed to the doctor's office, and then I went home and had therapy with Noah. I was honest with Noah. I told him I smoked at three thirty after the doctor's appointment, and we did a chain analysis, and we concluded that I had a high-emotion day and that emotion was frustration, which, in other words, anger turned inward is sadness. I just feel a very high amount of sadness that I don't think many people in this world do. And yet I know that I am not alone in this feeling as I have spoken to those in my life about mental health, and each person has a different point of view.

Some understand it because they have been through it themselves. Others don't get it because they either don't want to or they are too lazy to try to sit quietly without speaking, or judging, or trying to improve the moment. Sometimes you must sit in emotion as Noah would tell me. So here I am, being as raw as I can be because I know that, currently, the only person reading any of this is me and I am the one that is hurting. I am in pain—physically, mentally, emotionally, spiritually, and financially. And yet I am okay. I am alive. I am breathing, I am texting, I am laughing, I am enough. Today I am enough just the way I am, and the people in my life know me for me and love me for me. They are the people that I want to grow old with and spend my life with. They are the people who I call my family, and that is Book Club.

Book Club is my family, and I am proud and honored and touched to know and have known such amazing women. It is my life purpose to be surrounded by beautiful people inside and out! They have changed my life for the better. I am a better person because of these ladies—Natalie, Charlotte, Sarah, Susan, and Rachel, and, finally, Sheri. She was the glue that held us all together. She was the one that brought us all together. She is the one that we miss the most as she is no longer with us. She is in heaven, she is an angel, and she will always be with us. She will always be a part of this world if we are here and loving the way Sheri did is a gift and not a curse. She loved big, and she was born to smile and laugh. We miss you so much Sheri. RIP. The mother I never knew I needed.

It is 11:11. Make a wish. I wish things would change for the better. I hope for healing and peace and love. I wish that this world will be gentler with itself and remind those in it that life is a gift, a gift that is taken for granted by some. And I know I am one. That is why self-compassion is so important. It reminds you that you're not alone and there are others that are going through the same thing—if not, similar. Anyways I think this is a good place to stop as it is getting late and I haven't been sleeping, so we will see how this goes.

NATALIE KNOWS

November 13, 2023

It is 1:40 p.m., and I got off the phone with Sarah. She let me know that she told Natalie about the fact that I have been smoking again. I am not surprised that she told her. I had a feeling that she would. So now I must have a conversation with Natalie about the fact that I have been smoking again. So this week should be interesting. Today is eleven months since Sheri passed away, and I didn't even realize it until I looked at the date, and now I am feeling sad because it's sad that Sheri is not here anymore. And it's even sadder that I can't accept the fact that she killed herself when I am struggling with this out loudly daily and she gets to just be dead and leave all of us in shambles.

I can't think about her right now because I am trying to stay in the present moment. Currently, I am sitting in my living room; and I can see my Christmas tree, the fake fire, my water bottle, my phone, and my foot. I can hear the AC going in the next room, the fire crackling, the guy next door getting a tattoo. I can taste my water, and I can feel the table underneath my foot, and I am noticing that I am tired and overwhelmed. I am publishing this book. If not for me, then for whoever else needs to hear what I have to say. I am not going to be scared anymore. I am so tired of being afraid of everything. I am proceeding with the book and looking for a job and figuring out what I am going to do with the rest of my life.

And then God says, "Hey, remember me. I have my own plan for you. I know what is best for you." *So* here I leap, and here I have faith, and here is where I show the world just who you are because this is the beach within me. God is the only one, at the end of the day, to judge us. And his is the only love that I need. I don't know if I am supposed to be sober or not. I will know when I know and when I know you will know.

Katia Smith

Charlotte's Book Club Baby Shower

Saturday, December 2, 2023

After weeks of planning and me postponing the date, we were finally able to shower our Charlotte with love with patience as we await baby James. Today was perfect. It was my perfect day. Being surrounded by loved ones celebrating my best friend and her soon-to-be-son, James. Everyone dressed up. We put on some teatime hats, and we spilled the tea until the clock struck 4:00 p.m. It was a gathering of such amazing people, and those people are my family. May I introduce Book Club, my family—the family that loves me and accepts me and respects me. We have Sarah, Susan, Natalie, Rachel as the best fairy godmothers a child could ask for; Eddie as the godfather; and, of course, our angel, watching over us in heaven, Sheri. We missed you today, Sheri.

Well, I say we, but I am talking more about myself. I missed you today. And yet I know you were there because you are besides God in heaven, and you are helping him watch over all of us. The anniversary of your death is in eleven days, and I am still in shock that you are gone. It hurts my heart to know that we will have to wait so long to see you. At least I hope it's a while and yet I know that I will see you again. Because I believe you are happy right now and free and with my baby and your own son, Dominque. He needed his mamma, and you had to go, and you were needed in heaven, and so God took you home, where you belong.

I started my morning off by getting ready for the shower, and as I was getting ready, I checked my phone, and I double glanced as I had an email from Michael. I have a restraining order against him, and he has contacted me three times, so today was my last day reporting him. He is officially deleted and in police hands. I am done. Goodbye, Chapter Michael, and Hello, Baby James! I can't wait to meet you, my sweet boy. I am so excited to see you grow and see your mom be a mom.

I am sad that I do not have a child, but I do not know if I would have wanted a child. I had an abortion a few years back, and it has been having me thinking lately about the things I do want in my life: a partner that loves and respects me, a job I feel fulfilled in, and, lastly, a happy and healthy family and friends. Most of all, it makes me think of my own child in heaven with Sheri and if it knows that I love it and can't wait to meet it one day, but that day is not today.

Today was about Baby James and Charlotte. I can't wait to see your love blossom and see you as a mom, Charlotte. You are going to be such an amazing mom, and I will be alongside you help you every step of the way because you are my person and I love you with all my heart. You are the best friend a girl could ask for, and I am so honored and touched that God choose me to be James's aunt.

Today has been an emotional day, and I am lying in my bed typing this, and I have been having a panic attack in the last few hours. I have been practicing skills and talking to my DBT coach and talking to friends. I am hoping to sleep tonight. I haven't slept well in a few nights, and I hope I can eat tomorrow as I have also been struggling to do that. Tomorrow is a new day. New beginnings and a new day to create some memories with those that you love the most. Christmastime will never be the same again. As we welcome new life, we grieve the loss of Sheri. We are excited and sad at the same time. We cherish the memories we have with you, Sheri, and we will always remember you and be a part of us. That kind of love doesn't go away. It's energy that is passed on for generations. Today was a good day, but one of the saddest days of my life. And yet I am still standing and using my skills to get through the day—just like everyone else on this planet called Earth.

Day 1 of Sobriety

Tuesday, December 5, 2023

Today is December 5, 2023, and I am one day sober. I had been smoking weed for the last four days, and because I was smoking, it did not mix well with my medications that I am on for anxiety and depression. I hadn't slept much on those nights, and so finally I figured out the dosage on one of my medications was wrong. It was giving me so much stimulation that I wasn't able to sleep. I was smoking THC and was not able to sleep. I finally called the doctor, and we discussed what my options were to stop the 300mg all together and go from it for one day and then go back to 150mg the next day. By this time, I was so sleep deprived that I couldn't drive.

I guess I should back up a little bit to understand that I was on my way to my psychiatrist appointment on Wednesday night, and before I got there, I went to a smoke shop and picked up a pen. From that moment on until last night, I was using THC. I was high for four days straight, and I didn't sleep much during those four days. It wasn't until I couldn't feel safe to drive that I started asking for help. I reached out to my psychiatrist and explain to him that the dosage change he made was too much. I was so wired that I couldn't fall asleep. He knew I was also smoking THC. We planned together to take me off one medicine for one whole day and add the lower dose back the next day.

So that is exactly what we did. I continued to smoke the THC, I stopped taking the medicine, and I started paNatalieng. I couldn't drive and needed to be picked up. My psychiatrist prescribed Ativan.

It has the ability to help put me to sleep while also stopping the panic attacks from occurring to a higher level as I was already having suicidal ideations. I had no plan or interest in dying, and yet my mind had another plan. My mind was so checked out it didn't care if I lived or died. So I fought. I called my dad, who came to Natalie's house, and handed me a platter of tough love. He for sure ruined the high for me, and then he took me home, and I went to sleep. I went to sleep high last night since I physically for rid of my pen and gave it to Natalie since I have no self-control to get rid of it on my own. My dad wants me to quit *everything*, including nicotine. While I do want to, it is not possible right now. Right now, I can only take one thing away at a time. I am hoping he will understand and that this will not keep me out of the family dynamic.

I went onto a Zoom alumni meeting and shared about where I was and how I lapsed. I shared that I am ready to get back on the wagon and live a substance-free life. I can't promise I will do it for the rest of my life, but I can promise that just for today I will stay clean. For that I am very proud of myself advocating for myself with my doctors and therapist and even my own family and friends. I am hoping in time they will see the change and growth that I am making within myself. Even by writing this book, I am doing something for myself and no one else.

The things I have got through do not define me. All they have done has made me stronger. I am an ordinary woman who decided that she wanted to share her thoughts and emotions and journey with you in hopes that one day if life decides to hit you across the head, you will know you are not alone. Life can be beautiful, but it can also be painful, and for the year 2024, I am planning on seeing the beauty within the pain. I have so much happiness and excitement coming in the near 2024. I know the lessons, tears, screaming, and yelling that I did in 2023 will all be worth it. God has a way of showing us his plan right when we least expect it. So with that being said, I am closing the chapter to this year and saying hello to 2024!